my 2013

MISSION *Possible!*

Volume Four

Crystal,

Janet Guengy

Insight Publishing Company
Sevierville, Tennessee

Published by Insight Publishing Company
P.O. Box 4189
Sevierville, Tennessee 37864

Printed in the United States of America

ISBN 1-885640-92-7

MISSION *Possible!*

Radio Program

The exciting chapters in this volume of
Mission Possible! were taken from interviews
recorded for the *Mission Possible! Radio Program*
heard on select radio stations across America.

Each contributor was interviewed by
David E. Wright.

Alexandria Altman contributed to Mike Lattimore's interview.

Contents

A Message from the Publisher

Some ideas simply get better with time. *Mission Possible!* began as a promotional idea for professional speakers who were trying to expand their careers. Sharing the pages of a book with famous personalities like Stephen Covey, Mark Victor Hansen, and Bruce Jenner was a simple, but innovative strategy. One year later, *Mission Possible!* has taken on a life of its own and proven to be much more than a promotional tool.

What has become crystal clear to all of us who help publish *Mission Possible!* is that our contributing authors all have vibrant, life-changing messages. These professional speakers, trainers, and consultants are living "success stories." The counsel they give is based on real-world experience, not theory. And because each chapter is a transcribed interview, readers can have a personal encounter with each author, making the ideas presented even more relevant and entertaining.

Mission Possible! should be required reading for anyone wanting to grow and succeed. Regardless of the challenges you face in your career or personal life, the ideas, insights, and strategies presented by these dynamic personalities will make a difference for you. Don't miss a chapter in this exciting edition of *Mission Possible!* and watch for new editions coming soon!

Chapter 1

Bruce Jenner

After winning a gold medal in the 1976 Olympic Games, Bruce Jenner has gone on to winning seasons in life. He's known to millions as a motivational speaker, TV personality, sports commentator, commercial spokesperson, entrepreneur, actor and producer.

The Interview

David Wright (Wright)

Today we're talking to Bruce Jenner. Bruce captivated the world when he broke the world record by scoring 8,634 points in the decathlon at the 1976 Olympic games in Montreal and earned the title World's Greatest Athlete. In the years following his athletic achievements, Mr. Jenner has become a successful and highly respected motivational speaker, sports commentator, entrepreneur, commercial spokesperson, television personality, actor, producer, and author. Mr. Jenner serves on numerous advisory boards, such as the Special Olympics. He also serves on the Council of

Champions and the National Dyslexia Research Foundation. He is an avid supporter of Athletes and Entertainers for Kids. Mr. Jenner and his wife, Kris, serve on the board of the Dream Foundation, an organization that grants wishes to terminally ill adults. He has been a guest on *Oprah, The Tonight Show with Jay Leno,* and *Regis and Kathie Lee.* He is a highly regarded and successful author. His newest release is *Finding the Champion Within.* Bruce Jenner, welcome to *Mission Possible!*

Bruce Jenner (Jenner)

It's my pleasure; but you know that title, World's Greatest Athlete? It doesn't help my golf game!

Wright

I hear you're a ten handicap.

Jenner

Actually, I'm about a three or four right now. I've worked pretty hard on it; but when you're standing over that six-foot putt with six inches of break, titles don't seem to help—it keeps you pretty humble.

Wright

With all these titles—actor, athlete, spokesman, author—I read that you've been named Father of the Year by the U.S. Jaycees, and received the Father of the Year honors from the Southern California Father's Day Committee. Those are impressive honors.

Jenner

That's just because I have ten children. If you have ten children and you're still standing, boom! you get an immediate Father of the Year award. I've been very blessed in that department—six girls and four boys, ages twenty-three to four. I do the father thing every day, and I'm very lucky.

Wright

Those are great honors for a person whose time has been in such demand for years. Has family always been a number one priority for you?

Jenner

Definitely, especially in my type of business where you're out in the public. You get very plastic, very "surfacy." But your real life is with your family. That real life—taking the garbage out, carpools, relationships, good days, bad days, and on and on and on—is by far what I live with my family and the everyday stuff that I do. Then I get out there and motivate people and try to build some businesses.

Wright

While preparing for this interview, I got the feeling that a commitment to youth has always been important to you, especially the physically and mentally challenged. Is this a response to your own battle with dyslexia?

Jenner

Yes, because I can really identify with these kids. To be honest with you, being dyslexic myself, I always tell kids that if you're dyslexic and that's the only problem you have in life, you've got it made. You can deal with this thing. The bigger problem than being dyslexic is a lack of self-confidence in yourself, especially at a young age. When you're growing up and everybody's accelerating in school and doing well, and reading seems to be simple for everybody else, but for you perceptually picking those words up off the piece of paper is tough, you lose confidence in yourself. In my case, that's basically what I did. I lost interest in school; I flunked second grade; I didn't want to go to school. My biggest fear in life was to go to school, because I was afraid the teacher was going to make me read in front of the class. Not only perceptually did I have a hard time getting the words off the piece of paper, but also I got so emotionally upset because I didn't want to look bad in front of my friends. It just didn't work.

But it molded me into the type of person I am today. I always tell kids if I had not been dyslexic I would not have won the games, because being dyslexic made me special, made me different from everyone else. When I found what I call my little arena to play in, which happened to be sports, it became very important to me. I excelled at that. Not that later on down the line, after years and years of doing this, I always thought about the dyslexic thing, but that little dyslexic kid was always sitting in the back of my head outworking the next guy. I look at athletics in two ways: the athletic body and the athletic mind. I was given okay athletic skills physically; but being a kid who grew up with a lack of self-confidence, I found out my greatest gift was my athletic brain. I could outperform people under pressure because my brain worked so well, and I could come up with the performances when everyone else was dying. Dealing with pressure and fear and all those types of things you have to deal with, I was better at than anybody else. So it was an interesting metamorphosis through life.

Wright

Did anyone in your early years ever call you dumb or stupid?

Jenner

No, but I always felt dumb and stupid, because I was always in the slower classes in grade school growing up. Nobody had to say anything. It was more my own internal struggles that I was dealing with.

Wright

I talked to a good friend of yours, Billy Blades, the other day, and I also talked to Les Brown, who is a tremendous motivational speaker in the country. Both of these men told me the same story. They were dyslexic, and it almost devastated their childhood; they didn't find out about it until they were thirty-seven.

Jenner

I remember in junior high school one day they gave it a name and said, "You're dyslexic." I wondered if that was bad, if I was going to die from this. It was a pretty bad word. They said, "No, go back to class. Have a good day." That was about the extent of it back then. Actually, for a while it became too big a word. If any kid wrote anything backwards, they were dyslexic. It became a catch phrase for a lot of different problems. It's calmed down a little bit now. They've been able to analyze things like this. It's not the end of the world if you're dyslexic.

Remember the movie *City Slickers,* with Curly and Billy Crystal sitting by the fire? Billy Crystal asks Curly, the old wise cowboy, "What's the secret to life?" He says, "One thing," and the conversation continues. Finally, later on in the conversation, Billy Crystal asks, "What's that one thing?" Curly looks over and says, "That's for you to find out." That's so true. In life I was lucky at a young age to find this thing called sports. I found that I had an aptitude for that. That brought me out of my shell and helped me feel good about myself, which helped the self-confidence problems. The challenge for young kids today who are suffering with something like this is to find their niche in life. That's a parent's responsibility. It doesn't have to be in sports. It could be in a million different fields. Tom Cruise is dyslexic, and Cher—the list goes on and on and on of people who found their niche. I try to encourage kids to go out there and try art, try music, try acting, who knows? There is your talent. If it's taken away in one area, it's given to you in another. Your job is to find the other area and then go with it.

Wright

You have a new motivational book out titled *Finding the Champion Within,* published by Simon and Schuster. Tell us a little about it and who will benefit from reading it.

Jenner

I think everybody will. The reason I call it *Finding the Champion Within* is that when I was growing up, I never knew down deep in my soul if I had anything special down there. But every time I'd dig down deeper and deeper through athletics, which was testing me in competition all the time, I realized that there was something there, and I didn't even know what it was. Going through that long process and going through the games and being able to win and stand on top of the platform and all that—probably the one thing that gave me is confidence in people. We all have that champion that lives down deep inside that has the ability to overcome tremendous obstacles in our life and to do tremendous things with our life. But there's a process to finding that. With the book and through my speaking I talk about that process and try to motivate people to basically believe in themselves.

That's why I did the book. The speaking is kind of tough, because I run all over the United States to primarily sales forces, but also to all kinds of groups, and talk about finding the champion within. The travel's tough and you're away from home and all of that. But to me, I really enjoy the presentation. It took that performance in 1976 and that great journey that I was on, and it didn't die back then. It still lives on to help motivate people and to move people forward in their life. It may be one line, one sentence, one word within that might spark one person to say, "Hey, I do believe in myself, and I can do these things."

Wright

I remember reading a program that was produced by a company in Waco, Texas, called Success Motivation Institute, with a fellow named Paul Meyer. He did a program called "The Making of a Champion," and you were featured in one of the stories. It was very motivational. Wheaties has just commemorated its seventy-fifth anniversary, and you're back on the front of the box along with other superstar athletes like Tiger Woods and Michael Jordan. How does that feel after earning the title World's Greatest Athlete twenty-six years ago?

Jenner

To be honest with you, it's very flattering, mostly because when I got out of the games I went into the television world, the commercial world, and all the types of things I've been doing over the past years. It's very nice and very flattering to be in the top fifty athletes of the past decade and things like that. It's nice to have in my memory bank. I don't live on it or dwell on it in my own personal life, but it certainly is a nice position to be in. Obviously, I was very proud of that day, and it was a great day. I had trained for twelve years of my life for that moment, and I came through. I'm proud of that. It's a nice, very positive message when sometimes in our world today we need positive messages.

Wright

You're a highly respected motivational speaker today. What is the message that corporations want and need to hear in today's economy?

Jenner

You have to have a belief system. Two years ago we were riding high. Everything was just wonderful; everyone was making money; the stock market was going through the roof, on and on. Today we need to look at things probably more realistically than we did back then. We kind of had our heads in the sky. Today we have to be a lot more realistic; we can't just wander through life. Especially with 9/11 and all the things that we're going through in our country, we have to take life seriously. You get this great shot. You get seventy-five years, on average, that you're on this planet, and you've got to go for it. I always feel like everybody is at their best when they wake up in the morning and they're excited about that day, whether it's building a business, improving their relationship with their family, whatever it may be. When you get up in the morning, you've got to be excited about tackling that day, one day at a time. You constantly build on these days, day after day after day, and eventually you've really accomplished something. You've moved forward in your life. You've overcome a lot of things. Today you've got to be smart in what you're doing.

Wright

Did 9/11 have any impact specifically on your life or the life of your family?

Jenner

I think probably everybody knows somebody who was in those buildings and lost their life. We have one friend whose husband was in the building. She was eight months pregnant and daddy never came home. A month later she had the baby; she's a very close friend of ours. I think everybody is affected. You'd have to be a cold, heartless person not to be sitting there on the 11th of September and be affected. I was stuck in a hotel room in Milwaukee, sitting there all day long watching everything that was going on and just devastated by it.

The world changed that day. Our attitudes changed that day. It was a terrible, terrible tragedy, but I will say one thing: it certainly has brought our country together. It certainly has shown the world that we are not going to tolerate those types of things. You attack us and you've got big problems. We've shown a very strong hand, and I think our country is dealing with it very well. There's nothing wrong with a little bit of patriotism out there. We have the greatest country in the world, and I'm proud to be part of it.

Wright

When you're standing up there with the gold medal hanging around your neck and the band is playing our national anthem and the flag is going up, does that really have an impact on the rest of your life?

Jenner

It does have an impact on the rest of your life in the sense that forever you'll always be an Olympic champion. It's a pretty elite fraternity out there. That's the main thing that it does. When I went into the games I was the favorite; I was the world record holder. It was the last meet of my life. It was the last time I was ever going to do these things. But when I walked away I had accomplished everything in a sport I wanted to accomplish. I broke the world record three times, I had the Olympic record, I had the gold medal, number one in the world for three years. I walked away smiling because I was so happy that I could walk away accomplishing everything that I wanted to accomplish. Very few athletes can do that, walk away saying they did everything in the sport they could possibly do. It was a great career, and now I'm moving on.

In my sport there was no longevity to it. I don't go to my friends and say, "Are we going to go throw the shot or pole vault today?" No, we're going to go play golf. It wasn't like Tiger Woods, after he won the Masters, throwing his golf clubs away and never touching a golf club the rest of his life. I had to do that. I had to walk away from my best friend. But I knew that, and I knew that going in. Was it hard? Yes, it was hard. I was the best in the world at what I did. It's kind of like a piano player, who for twelve years of his life sits in front of that piano banging out that music. You get your chance, you go in front of the rest of the world, you play the most beautiful music the world's ever heard, and when the song's over, you put your hands in your pockets and you never touch the piano again.

That was kind of sad from my stance. It was a bittersweet kind of moment. It was great and satisfying to win, but I was also sad I was leaving my best friend. It was kind of an interesting thing to go through. I realized the reason I was walking away. Roger Bannister had a quote about sports and life; he said, "Only in something like running can finality be achieved, but it is not the type of finality that leaves you with nothing to live for, because sport is not the main aim in life. Yet to achieve perfection in one area, however small, makes it possible to face uncertainties in the more difficult problems in life." That's a great quote. That's what sports is all about: go in there, compete hard, and then move on in life to the more important things.

Wright

I'm old enough to remember Roger Bannister.

Jenner

He was the first man to break four minutes in the mile.

Wright

Some of the greatest athletes in the world have taken up golf. Michael Jordan is an example. He would rather play golf than basketball. Why is that?

Jenner

It's just a very challenging game. I play on what's called a Celebrity Players Tour. I played one event this weekend up in Las Vegas. There were about eighty guys. They call it the Celebrity Players Tour, but it's probably ninety-five percent retired athletes. It's just a great game. Even when you get a little older, you still enjoy the competition, the competitive spirit, the camaraderie with all the other guys that are out there. It's a difficult and frustrating game. It looks so simple, but it's so difficult to do. It's a great challenge. It's a totally different pace than what you're used to. In my days of competing, I was in the Olympic arena. I was out there grunting and groaning in training. Golf's just the opposite. You're out there with your friends; you're enjoying the game; it's a beautiful day. You're on a golf course—a highly competitive, difficult sport, and it makes it fun. You can do it the rest of your life. It's not like you have to give it up in a few years because your knees go. In most cases, you can do it until you're seventy.

Wright

My brother was a golf instructor and he took me out. I was a weekend duffer and couldn't play at all. I just went for the fun. He got me out one day with nothing but a nine iron and knocked twenty-five strokes off my game. He told me to throw the rest of them away and just keep that one.

Jenner

He was smart; he knew what he was doing.

Wright

With our *Mission Possible!* talk show and book, we are trying to encourage people in our audience to be better, live better, and be more fulfilled by listening to the examples of our guests. Is there anyone or anything in your life that has made a difference for you and helped you become a better person?

Jenner

You have to pick the number one person in your life, and that's my wife, Kris. We've been very blessed with a lot of children. We've been married a long time now. That's your soul mate, the person you spend every day with. That's who you talk with about everything. So number one would be my wife. We're very fortunate and have been blessed in a lot of ways. By far, my wife. She's been the best—my bud!

Wright

She works with you now, doesn't she?

Jenner

Yes, she runs the offices. She keeps me organized—too organized, I think!

Wright

I was reading about an old track coach of yours, L.D. Weldon, who is credited with having been the first person to really recognize the great potential that you obviously showed later on. Was he a mentor of sorts?

Jenner

To be honest, I'd almost have to consider L.D. as my second dad. I lived in his home in college. He asked me to come out to this little dinky school in Iowa in the late sixties. When you're eighteen to twenty-two, there are a lot of things going on in your life. He was a great human being to be around. He was a great person with good moral standing, good guidance, just a great person to be around. He was a character. L.D. always liked multi-eventers, and he actually had recruited me to play football. I lasted about three weeks and had to have knee surgery, so that was a short career. Fortunately, it was the best injury I ever had, because it got me out of that sport. He was not the technical coach that just sat there and worked on technique; he was a motivator. He'd help you out with as much technique as I think he was possible of doing, but he was such a great guy and such a great motivator that you didn't want to lose races because you didn't want to let L.D. down. He's had great decathlon guys in the past. He was sixty-five when we met, and he'd had a guy in the 1936 Olympic games. His name was Jack Parker, and he took the bronze medal in Berlin.

To be honest with you, my favorite picture that I have is a picture of L.D. standing there with his fist clenched and he's got his hat on. He always used to brag about every athlete he ever had. We had to listen to every story about every athlete, but he signed this picture, "To Bruce, the greatest athlete I ever coached. L.D. Weldon." To me, knowing L.D. was a really, really big deal. That was very special. He was a great human being and great for those years from eighteen to twenty-two for guidance and that type of thing.

Wright

I remember as a kid seeing Burt Lancaster play Jim Thorpe, the all-American. I jumped every hedge on the way home from the theater. It motivated me.

Jenner

Oh, yeah, I remember that. They did Jim Thorpe. They did Bob Mathias, a story on his life. When I started running the decathlon— 1970 was my first one—I didn't even think about the Olympics. The reason I got so excited about it is that the guys in the past who had won the Olympic decathlon were not just Olympic champions, they almost became part of American history. Jim Thorpe, Bob Mathias, Rafer Johnson—these guys were bigger than life, because it was such a tough event. That was one of the motivating factors. To be honest with you, as I got closer and closer to the games, I didn't care what happened. I just wanted to stand on the same stage as a Rafer Johnson, Toomey, Mathias, or all these guys in the past who had won it. It's a tough deal to win.

Wright

After seeing the movie, I read the life story of Bob Matthias. I just couldn't believe it. Have you ever met him?

Jenner

He's a great friend and a great human being.

Wright

What do you think makes up a great mentor? In other words, are there characteristics that mentors seem to have in common?

Jenner

Yes. First of all they have to be giving people. A mentor has to be, I think, of great moral character. I think that's extremely important. It's like what is called the MasterMind Principle. You find out what you do and what you want to become in life, and you go and associate with those people that are doing it. That's extremely strong; having somebody in your life who has been through experiences, who is willing to help you, is extremely important. You are a lot of what your surroundings are. It's important to find those people out and associate yourself with those types of people, from your family, your parents, the kids you hang out with, the other adults you hang out with. Things like that, growing up, are extremely important. Who are the people that you're looking up to? That's important in life.

Wright

You've influenced so many people around you. I've talked to your daughter a few times. Does she work in your company?

Jenner

Yes, four years of paying for college and she works for us! She started for us four years ago, but she's looking at other options now, so I don't know how long she'll hang out with us.

Wright

Most people are fascinated with the new TV shows about being a survivor. What has been the greatest comeback you have made from adversity in your career or life?

Jenner

Overcoming the dyslexic problem would probably be it. The old saying, "Success is not measured by heights attained, but by obstacles overcome." Little things like, for me, my biggest fear was going to school because I was afraid the teacher was going to make me read in front of the class. I hated that. I sat there with sweaty palms all day long in fear that it was going to happen. Cut to years later. I go to the games, I win the games, I get a job. It's one of the first things they have you do—teleprompter work. I panic. That little dyslexic kid is there. But I was able to go out there and find my own ways to get around it, to be able to do those kinds of things. I used to host *Good Morning America* when David Hartman or one of the others was gone. That was two hours of teleprompter reading, on and on. For me, I overcame more to do that than I did to win the games.

Little things like that along the way. I have to say I really lost interest in a lot of things in the middle eighties. Then I met my wife. We got married eleven years ago, and being with somebody you love gives you more reason to work. It's not just about working for yourself. I didn't care that much about it; I hadn't worked for years. But finding somebody and renewing the family, adding more kids on to the family, starts to kick you in the butt. I had to start getting serious about life again. It's not just about little old me, because I don't need that much. But now I've got a family and a four-year-old and a six-year-old. It motivates you to get back out there and get some things going.

Wright

When you consider the choices you have made down through the years, has faith played an important role in your life?

Jenner

To a point. I believe in God and go to church, not regularly, but I go. I believe God gave me a life, gave me some talents, to do with what I can. And then the rest is up to me. My success or failure is going to be determined by myself. I take personal responsibility for my life, and I've always felt that. I've always felt like I had God-given talents, good points and bad points. My job is to use those things, to get out there and make something of myself. To wake up in the morning and feel good about myself is my responsibility. I can't say, "Oh, I failed and it was God's will." No, I failed and it was my problem. Or, "I was successful, and it was in the glory of God." I always feel like I worked hard. God gave me some talent, and I'm the one who worked hard, and if He's looking down on me and saying, "You did a good job," that's all I need.

Wright

In reading about you, I was interested in the Longevity Network. Are you still involved in that?

Jenner

Yes, we're a network marketing company based in Henderson, Nevada. We sell all kinds of products. We've been doing this for eight or nine years.

Wright

Is it all health related?

Jenner

We do health-related stuff; we do hair care products, all kinds of stuff for home-based business entrepreneurs. We have vitamin programs, weight loss programs, all sorts of stuff.

Wright

I interviewed Dr. Mindell the other day, and he was talking about the health revolution. It was like a war to him. He said each year about 140,000 Americans die from adverse effects from prescription drugs, and almost one million are injured due to dispensing errors. He said people are going to have to take control of their own life and their own health in terms of vitamins, running, exercising, and those sorts of things.

Jenner

I certainly agree with that. We have to take responsibility, and again it comes down to it's our responsibility to take care of our health and eat properly. Honestly, it's not that difficult. It just has to be a priority. Sometimes we don't take our health seriously until something goes wrong. Then it's the wake-up call. Eating properly, to me, is the 80/20 Theory. Eighty percent of the time you eat what normally you would think of as good food; the other twenty percent, have fun. Have a little Häagen-Dazs, a little of this and that; you can have a little fun with those things. But eighty percent of the time you have to eat right. Then you can kind of splurge and have a good time.

Exercise is interesting. The CDC came out with a study back in '96, I think it was, basically saying that living a sedentary lifestyle is as hazardous to your health as if you smoke. That's pretty scary, but that's the bad news. The good news was that a moderate amount of exercise, just a little bit of exercise, has as positive effect on your health as if you're a marathoner. So the good news here is that a little bit goes a long ways. That's an important study. A lot of the reason people don't exercise is that if they're living a relatively sedentary lifestyle, they think doing exercise is like running the 10K, because that's what they see people doing. They say, "I could never do that." But can they walk up three flights of stairs instead of taking the elevator? You certainly can do that. Just doing a little and realizing that you don't have to run marathons or go to the gym five times a week—you just have to live an active lifestyle. Get as much exercise in your daily life as you can. If you're in an apartment, or your office is on the fifth floor, don't take the elevator—walk up. Everybody always looks for the closest parking place for the grocery store. Find one that's far away and walk. There are a lot of ways just to get some activity in your life, which is going to have a very positive effect on your health.

Wright

Speaking of health, I remember reading about something you had created called Personal Blood Storage, Inc. What is that all about?

Jenner

Back in the late eighties, early nineties a friend came to me and said he was staring this business called Personal Blood Storage. Basically, what he had developed was the technology to store blood at 70° C below zero. They had been able to freeze blood because it's an individual cell freezing process instead of like an organ, which if you try to freeze is cell on cell, and it breaks itself up and doesn't work very well. At least not yet; they'll probably figure it out someday. But they've been freezing blood for years. The problem was they didn't have freezer capacity; they only had small freezers. So he developed this technology which he was going to take out and do personal blood storage. It was a very interesting entrepreneurial effort. The concept was so much better than the blood banks that are out there now. In each freezer we could do about 45,000 units of blood. The blood system in the United States doesn't freeze. The Red Cross is a monopoly, and it doesn't freeze blood, so every thirty days it has to turn over the blood supply. That's why they're constantly asking. I can tell you, the first two weeks of January the Red Cross will be on the news saying that we need blood because for the last month, because of the holidays, nobody's been giving blood, so the system is out and there's no reserve of blood. So Personal Blood Storage was the ability for you to put your own blood away if you wanted to. Over a year's period you could put four or five pints of blood away, store it, and if you ever needed it, it's there so you have your own blood. Or you could start to build up a reservoir, a supply of blood that's on the side, so in case of a tragedy you would always have blood available. Well, the Red Cross is a monopoly. The poor guy spent a lot of money and got shut down every place he went. It was ruthless. The Red Cross came after us because they didn't want the competition. So after about five years of spending a lot of money and trying to fight the Red Cross in every trench, he finally said he'd had enough.

Wright

The reason I was so interested in it is that just last week someone was telling me that if I ever needed any kind of surgery and had some time before I had the surgery, to always go in and donate my own blood so there would be no rejection. Is that the basic principle?

Jenner

Yes, it's your blood. Why would you want to put somebody else's blood in there if you could use your own blood? The concept for it was fabulous, except you're going up against a monopoly.

Wright

It's encouraging that you still go mountain biking, run on the track at Pepperdine, play golf, are a commercially rated pilot, and race cars professionally in the Grand Prix events. That's pretty cool.

Jenner

I live a very active life and I enjoy doing a lot of things. That's why I was a decathlon guy.

Wright

If you could have a platform and tell our audience something you feel would help or encourage them, what would you say?

Jenner

Four words, the keys to success in life: gamble, cheat, lie, and steal! *Gamble*—gamble your best shot in life. Dare to take risks. Life has got to be a great adventure or it's nothing. *Cheat*—cheat those who would have you be less than you are. Surround yourself with positive people, uplifting people, people who want to see you do well. Turn around and help them and you're truly a champion. *Lie*—lie in the arms of those that you love. When it comes right down to it, all we have is one another. Never take the love that you give or the love that you receive for granted. Finally, *steal*—steal everyone with happiness. Live every day as if it's your last, because we never know when that day is going to come. Gamble, cheat, lie, and steal.

Wright

That's great advice from a great American.

We have been talking today to Bruce Jenner, who literally captivated us all when he broke the world record in 1976 in the Olympic Games, and he's still at it, as we have just found out. He's not only an athlete but a great business person and a much requested speaker.

Mr. Jenner, we really appreciate you being with us today on *Mission Possible!* It's been a personal privilege for me.

Jenner

It was a lot of fun. It was great having a chance to talk to you.

www.brucejenner.com

Chapter 2

Mike Lattimore

Mike Lattimore is America's Digital Defender and the CEO of Appleseeds Across America, a community digital empowerment project to create information technology jobs for America's youth. He is the author of Who's Watching Your Computer? *and a technology advocate who is helping to build regional IT training partnerships across the country. Mike's topics include* Identity Theft: Will I Be Next? *and* Keeping Kids Safe Online.

The Interview

David E. Wright (Wright)

Today we are talking with Mike Lattimore, a dynamic and passionate speaker who is also a computer security whiz. His varied background includes careers as an animal trainer, an entertainment photographer for such stars as Michael Jackson, a game show casting co-coordinator and television producer, marketing director, and most recently, a computer scientist for a major utility company. Today he is known as the "Digital Defender." Mike Lattimore, welcome to *Mission Possible!*

Mike Lattimore (Lattimore)

Thank you very much, Dave.

Alexandria Altman (Altman)

Welcome, Mike.

Lattimore

Thank you, too, Alexandria.

Wright

Mike, can you tell us a little about what you do as the Digital Defender?

Lattimore

Sure, David. My mission as the Digital Defender is to help bridge the digital divide by advocating technology training opportunities for the youth of America. My role is to help create sustainable models for regional information technology training partnerships in communities across the nation. So I create computer labs and help organizations to foster those labs so that they can become training grounds for young people and displaced workers.

Wright

What is the digital divide?

Lattimore

The digital divide is a condition in which technology separates or disempowers people.

As you know, technology can be an excellent tool for bringing us together, for connecting us on many levels. For example, we can use e-mail to instantly connect with anyone on the planet. So we are now looking at our world as a global village rather than the big world that we were in thirty years ago. Conversely, technology can disempower us when people do not have access to technology careers, when they do not have access to computer literacy skills. Then they become afraid of technology, intimidated by it, and disempowered, both economically and spiritually.

Altman

Mike, what actual damage can hackers do if they get into corporations' computer files?

Lattimore

That's a very interesting perception, Alexandria. Actually, my take on it is that hackers are not, by definition, necessarily bad people. Hackers are actually a very necessary entity because they control technology. It is important that we have individuals who can control technology; otherwise, technology will control us. The problem is when the hacker crosses the moral boundary line and becomes ethically challenged. By that I mean they begin to work for the Dark side rather than the Force. So when a hacker begins to compromise the integrity of data, begins to compromise authentication methods, like passwords, and damages data and systems, then that hacker is, by definition, a cracker. So I just wanted to clear that up. The media's perception is that all hackers are bad, and that's not necessarily so. There are, indeed, hackers who are helpers.

Altman

Is there real espionage, or simply people trying to mess up files and create more work for the employees?

Lattimore

Yes, there are individuals who, as I mentioned, are ethically challenged and who have a personal vendetta against large corporations, possibly like Microsoft, or government agencies and that sort of thing. They dwell in the Dark places, doing damage and creating viruses and malicious code, like Trojan horses, that wreak havoc on people's computer systems. And many times it is innocent people who get hurt.

Wright

Mike, let's change the subject for a minute. I read that you competed in Toastmasters International's World Championship of Public Speaking. What was that like?

Lattimore

That was awesome! It was an experiment in intuition. All along the way, I had no intention of going to the top. But it was revealed to me that when I take the time to become still and allow intuition to flow through me, messages of truth will come. In this instance, those messages turned out to be speeches, and they were universal messages that actually spoke to me personally. One of them was about the call to passion—living your life with the passion that you were born with, that you came here with. The other was about never forgetting that thing inside of you that calls to you. Each of us has that call, David. That championship experience revealed to me what my call is. It's the gift of communication, the gift of connecting with people, touching people. So in that aspect, it was truly an experiment in intuition.

Altman

You are a champion of youth causes. Tell us a little bit about how you interact with youth and the different ways you reach them.

Lattimore

Primarily, as the Digital Defender, I foster computer technology access labs. These are places where kids can come and learn more about computers, where they can hone their skills, look for jobs, and socialize. The thing that happened for me many years ago was that someone took the time to come to my school. I grew up in a neighborhood called Woodlawn, on the South Side of Chicago, during the sixties, a very turbulent time. A gentleman named Rev. Christopher Moore came to my school when I was about nine years old, and he drafted me, so to speak, into the Chicago Boys' Choir. In doing so, he sparked a flame inside of my heart, introducing me to another side of life, and taught me that there was something that I had inside of me that connected to other people. So today my mission is to help young people find that spark inside of themselves, because I believe it is when we are young that the passion is burning so brightly. It's as we start to get older that we kind of let those flames die down. So I use technology, sometimes even computer games, to get people involved with computer systems and technology.

Altman

You almost remind me of Meteor Man. Did you see that show?

Lattimore

Yes, that was a great show. As you might can tell by my moniker, the Digital Defender, I love superheroes. The Digital Defender is a metaphor for the hero that's inside of all of us.

Wright

You realize that the Chicago Boy's Choir is world famous, don't you?

Lattimore

Yes, indeed. They are now known as Chicago Children's Choir, and they have performed all over the world. And the amazing thing, David, is that no matter where they sing, no matter what language they're singing in, the people who listen to them are touched. The tears flow whether it's in the Slavic languages, Afrikaans, French, or German. It doesn't matter—it's in the language of the heart.

Wright

I have a thirteen-year-old daughter, Mike. She surfs through that Internet and moves the mouse around at the speed of light, which frustrates her daddy immeasurably, because I'm supposed to be the smart one. Do you find that kids are really much better at learning computer programs and using computers than adults?

Lattimore

I think so, Dave. I think that our youth today are resonating at a different frequency than we were as kids. When I was a kid, our big thing was running around the neighborhood ringing doorbells. The kids today don't have the same opportunities for social interaction, so many of them are forced to use technology for their social relationships. That's exactly how hackers, sometimes young kids ten or eleven years old, are recruited. Since they revere heroes, when they get on-line it's the hackers and crackers, the ones who command that power of technology, that they admire and revere. So many times these kids are solicited into relationships with some of these ethically challenged individuals and they learn how to steal passwords, among other things. Then they graduate on to learning how to illegally obtain credit card numbers, and later they may even learn how to steal identities (which is, incidentally, a million-dollar business) Before they know it, they're working for the Dark side and they can't get out.

Wright

Recently my daughter had fourteen seventh-graders over to our house for a sleepover for her birthday party. I kept saying, "You'd better get on the telephone and call all your friends," and she just looked at me like I was kind of stupid and said that she had e-mailed them all in less than a minute. All fourteen of them showed up.

Lattimore

Exactly; it's the instant messaging service that they use now. All of them went to instant messaging.

Wright

And her homework, I'll have to admit, has been a lot better too.

Lattimore

Yes indeed. They don't want to wait for e-mail so they just click the instant messenger and the message shows up in real time. It's an interesting statement about the paradigm that we're in, because it used to be that belief systems took years to travel around the globe. Right now our kids are involved in a paradigm, or world view, in which belief systems shift literally almost overnight. A computer virus that hits one computer in my sleepy little town of Altadena can now travel the globe in under seventy-two hours. Messages can travel the planet, movement can now sweep the globe. The events of September 11 illustrate the power of technology to change our thinking. So our kids are standing in the middle of a new kind of power. They need guidance and training on how to wield this power as they step into their own as the leaders of the twenty-first century. That is my mission: to be one of the angels, one of the mentors, to be there for them.

Wright

Mike, would you explain what Appleseeds Across America does?

Lattimore

Sure, Dave. Appleseeds Across America is a project that was born because I have always loved the story of Johnny Appleseed. When I first heard that story, I was about six years old, and I was impassioned by the vision of seeing this man travel the entire country dropping apple seeds wherever he went, knowing one day an apple tree would stand where he left that seed. That, to me, was just the most awesome vision. As I grew up to became a computer scientist, I realized that I had the capability and the potential of being able to plant the seed of technology in young people's minds, in their hearts. And maybe one day they would go on to coach other youngsters, and soon we'd have a generation of empowered youths, leading us into a technologically empowered future. And so Appleseeds Across America was born out of that vision. Basically, what we do is create computer technology access labs. We call this effort "Let's Bring Back the Neighborhood!" These neighborhood computer labs are places where senior citizens can go and learn to surf the Internet, how to use the keyboard, and even make friends with the mouse. It's a place where youngsters can hang out and have social interaction with other kids. People who are displaced can actually go and learn new job skills for low or no cost. In this manner we help our neighbors take advantage of the technology revolution.

Altman

Mike, with our *Mission Possible!* talk show and book, we're trying to encourage people in our audience to be better, live better and be more fulfilled by listening to the examples of our guests. Is there anyone in your life who has made a difference for you and helped you to be a better person?

Lattimore

Yes, there are a number of people, Alexandria. So many of them, I couldn't start to mention them. But there is one individual that I need to mention because I talk about him incessantly, and that is the Rev. Christopher Moore. He was the founder of the Chicago Children's Choir. This man took the time out of his life to come into a troubled, inner-city neighborhood and to handpick kids and give them something that they didn't have. I'll never forget the day he selected me to join the choir. I told him, "But I can't sing!" He said, "Use your imagination and just imagine what it would be like if you could sing. How would you sound? How would you feel?" So this man nurtured me until I found myself being a first soprano, and standing at the lead of the choir. He created a reverberation in the lives of many that I work with today, by taking the time to make a difference in just one person's life. That reminds me of the story of the starfish, and the little kid flinging the starfish back into the ocean. Some guy tells him, "Hey, there are millions of them." And the little kid says, "Yes, but it made a difference to that one!"

Wright

What do you think makes up a great mentor, Mike? In other words, are there characteristics that mentors seem to have in common? You mentioned time with the choir director. Are there other characteristics that are important?

Lattimore

Yes, David, I think that the character asset of humility is very valuable, particularly in today's climate. Humility to me is being teachable. That means when I accept the responsibility of being a mentor, I am willing to learn with this young person, because they can teach me a lot about how to be an effective leader, how to be a better listener, how to be a better evaluator, and how to allow an individual to learn from their mistakes. There is just no other way to learn sometimes. It's almost like drinking tea. You can tell someone what it tastes like, but they'll never know until they pick up the cup and taste it for themselves.

Altman

Mike, when you consider the choices you've made down through the years, has faith played an important role in your life?

Lattimore

That's an excellent question. There were times in my life when I actually felt that I had lost my faith. There were many dark nights of the soul in some of my younger years, and during those years I wondered if I would ever be able to come back. There were individuals who went to the places that I went and never returned. However, somewhere, deep inside, there was a glimmer of hope, like a little voice telling me to just hold on, because help was on the way! Somehow I became open to that guidance, and through a strange turn of events, which I recognize now as spiritual experiences—although I didn't recognize them then—I began to be moved, led, directed, and inspired to make the right choices in my life. One day I woke up from what had appeared to be a nightmare existence, and I looked in the mirror and said, "What happened to you?" I had undergone a human revolution, and I believe that that is the key of true change on our planet. It's not, in my opinion, necessarily a revolution that happens in our society, or a revolution that happens in our government, but it's a human revolution—it's something that happens inside of us that makes the most impact in our transformation of this planet. And I believe that that sort of revolution is contagious. When it happens inside an individual, and it happens on a true level, it will create a true awakening in another human being. That is the essence of transformational leadership, and that has been my experience. It is the substance of my existence here. So yes, faith has definitely been the cornerstone of my evolution.

Wright

Mike, you're around schools a lot, dealing with kids for many causes and reasons, do you feel they are getting the lessons in faith that we did growing up?

Lattimore

That's interesting, David. You know, I think not. I think that we live in a world that we (meaning the people of our generation) have never seen before. I don't think that we really are empowered to step into our roles in knowing what we know and doing what it is we do. See, we were raised right. A favorite saying in my part of town was, "My mama didn't raise no fool." She taught me the difference between right and wrong, and sometimes it's a challenge for us to step into that role as being the leader, the guide, the mentor, the supporter of our young people. And they are looking to us so desperately for that. We're time-challenged, David. We live in an instant society driven by technology. We want fast food, instant potatoes—we want everything right now. It's really a challenge for us to stop and take the time to participate in the healing of our youngsters. They desperately need us.

Wright

Someone asked me recently why I went to church every Sunday. I told them it didn't have anything to do with God; I was going to have to pass my mother when I went to heaven. I didn't want to explain to her why I missed.

Lattimore

That's good. My best friend often says, "I don't think that prayer changes God's mind, but it certainly changes my mind."

Wright

Most people in our culture are fascinated by the new TV shows about being a survivor. What has been the greatest comeback you have made from adversity in your career or in your life?

Lattimore

I grew up during a very turbulent time. There was gang warfare, intense gang warfare, going on in the Southside of Chicago during the time I was growing up. I got a chance to see some of the most brutal and cruel behavior that you could ever imagine. Although it was a terrifying time for me, I had a choice. The choice was that I could become a part of that scenario or I could seek something else. I knew that there had to be a way out and that somehow, because I was very devoutly spiritual as a child, as most children are, I put out a call. I asked the angels, I asked God, whoever it was out there, to reveal himself and to help me.

And what happened was that people began to appear in my life: Christopher Moore, my godfather; some of the people from the Kuumba workshop who got me involved in street theater during my "hippie" days. They allowed me to channel those chaotic energies and turn them into something positive. They helped me transform into becoming a part of the solution, rather than a part of the problem. There was a fire that was burning inside of me, and these angels, I call them, came along and started to fan those smoldering embers until it became a flame. Today that passion is still alive inside of me, and everyone who knows me gets to share in it!

Wright

Did you have great family support?

Lattimore

Yes indeed—my mother, who gave me an early belief in Goodness, and in the Unseen. Also my extended family and friends who continue to support me in Love and in Spirit. There were also people in my life, I believe, who were angels but were walking the earth in human form. I believe that. And I think that we are not really aware of those people until after they are gone, when they've left this place. We look back and say, "That person truly was an angel in my life." So those are the people who pulled me through when I could not make it on my own. I can never pay these people back, but I believe in "paying forward " by helping others.

Altman

I believe that, too, Mike. If you could have a platform and tell our audience something you feel that would help or encourage them, what would you say?

Lattimore

I would say exactly what has been said to me and through me in my talks to young people, that there is something alive inside of you, deep down inside, just waiting for you to remember it. It's been calling ever since you were a little kid. When people used to bend over to you and ask, "What are you going to be when you grow up?" and you'd say, "An astronaut . . . a scientist . . . I'm going to be a minister . . . a preacher." You believed in magic. You believed that you could just speak the Word and it would happen. I believe that all of us are being called to remember that essence inside of us. When we see individuals—world famous entertainers that we're amazed at, like Michael Jackson, who my family watched the other night. When we see those people and our hearts jump, we are reminded that this, too, lives in us. So I would advise people to take time in the stillness, to make sacred space and go and look for that Thing that is inside of them, waiting for them to remember it. And when they do, they will come alive with an Energy that they never thought existed.

Altman

There is a saying, and I don't know if I can quote it correctly: "It takes a lifetime to grow up; it only takes a moment to come back as a child."

Lattimore

That is so true. You know, one of my big secrets is that when I was a kid, I swore I'd never grow up. I said I don't care if I'm looking older than grandpa, I'm not going to grow up. I held true on my promise. My kids make sure of that. I keep in mind a favorite phrase from a Children's Choir song which goes, "Remember the things that gave you joy when you were young; remember the things that made you laugh, made you sing, made you dance; Think on these things, for they are true. . . ."

Wright

I was really interested in something you had written about the Rev. Christopher Moore. You called him a mentor, an angel, on this program. Let me read it to you, "Whenever I think about the phenomenal impact this man's vision had on this world, I am moved to tears. People need to know that when they support the vision of the CCC, they are building and healing lives all over the planet." This man must have really made an impact on you.

Lattimore

He did; he did. Christopher taught me the Power of One. When I was a small boy, I thought to myself, "What difference can I make? It's such a big world. There's so much danger out there; how can I ever make a difference?" Christopher taught me to stand on a stage in front of thousands of people and to open my mouth and let this power move through me. When I heard what came out of me, I realized it was something above and beyond me, that I could not do this alone. What it did, it taught me that I can create a similar awakening in another human being.

This something inside of me wants to connect to others, to uplift them and help them, for they, too, have walked through the dark meadows of the soul, just as I have. They, too, have felt afraid and alone and unable to do anything. "Because I'm only one person," says the Ego. And it's not true. We are the Ones that we've been waiting for. In all these years, we've waited for someone else to come along and awaken us to what's inside of us, when all along, like Dorothy in *The Wizard of Oz,* we never left home.

Wright

I know you do a lot of volunteer work with kids. Specifically, you do a lot of career days at school. What do you say to young people about their careers? Do you give them advice, listen to them?

Lattimore

I talk with them. My motive is to listen, to inspire, and to let them know about the wealth of technology careers that are available. Many think that the only computer career is programming. I let them know about careers in network security, network engineering, web design, graphic design, 3D animation, video editing, and music production, to name a few. There are absolutely hundreds of different IT career paths, so I get them excited.

Then I have them start doing some possibility thinking. What is it that you really like to do? Do you like to create things? Do you like helping people, or do you like fixing things? We start walking down those possibility paths. I give them a list of resources, like technology centers in their community where they can go to get experience or training. I try to create linkages, get other mentors that I know, actually professionals, fired up who can go into these schools and make contact and become a resource connector for them. So my job is to go in and get them riled up and started with possibility thinking. Soon they're thinking, "Yeah, maybe I can be a scientist like Mike." And when they step over that line, from saying "Maybe I could" to "YES, I CAN!" then the next step is taking some action. My job is to be there for them, to assist them in doing that.

Wright

Well, Mike, this thirty minutes has just flown by.

Lattimore

It sure has, David.

Wright

We appreciate your being a guest on our program today.

Lattimore

I appreciate what you're doing, too, David. It's certainly needed.

Wright

Today we have been talking to Mike Lattimore, a dynamic, passionate speaker, a computer whiz, and, as we have found out in the last thirty minutes, a man who really loves to deal with and help other people, especially children. Thank you so much, Mike.

Lattimore

Thank you, David. Thank you, Alexandria. What you do is greatly appreciated.

Altman

And you are a great inspiration.

Lattimore

Thank you. You guys have a blessed day.

Mike Lattimore
America's Digital Defender
P.O. Box 238
Altadena, CA 91001-0238
Hotline: (626) 399-4238
Fax/voicemail: (626) 296-8455
E-mail: speaker@digitaldefender.org
www.digitaldefender.org

Chapter 3

Jack Canfield

In addition to being the founder and co-creator of Chicken Soup for the Soul®, Jack is the founder of Self-Esteem Seminars, which trains entrepreneurs, educators, corporate leaders, and employees how to accelerate the achievement of their personal and professional goals. Jack is also the founder of the Foundation for Self-Esteem, located in Culver City, California, which provides self-esteem resources and training to social workers, welfare recipients and human resource professionals.

The Interview

David E. Wright (Wright)

Today we are talking to Jack Canfield. You probably know him as the founder and co-creator of the *New York Times* number one best-selling *Chicken Soup for the Soul* book series, which currently has thirty-five titles and fifty-three million copies in print in over thirty-two languages. Jack's background includes a B.A. from Harvard, a master's degree from the University of Massachusetts, and an honorary doctorate from the University of Santa Monica. He has been a high school and university teacher, a workshop facilitator, a psychotherapist, and for the past twenty-five years a leading authority in the area of self-esteem and personal development. Jack Canfield, welcome to *Mission Possible!*

Jack Canfield (Canfield)

Thank you, David. It's great to be with you.

Wright

I talked with Mark Victor Hansen a few days ago. He gave you full credit for coming up with the idea of the *Chicken Soup* series. Obviously, it's made you an internationally known personality. Other than recognition, has the series changed you personally—and if so, how?

Canfield

I would say that it has, and I think in a couple of ways. Number one, I read stories all day long of people who've overcome what would feel like insurmountable obstacles. For example, we just did a book, *Chicken Soup for the Unsinkable Soul.* There's a story in there about a single mother with three daughters. She got a disease and had to have both of her hands and both of her feet amputated. She got prosthetic devices and was able to learn how to use them so she could cook, drive the car, brush her daughters' hair, get a job, etc. I read that and I think, "What would I ever have to complain and whine and moan about?" So I think at one level it's just given me a great sense of gratitude and appreciation for everything I have, made me less irritable about the little things. I think the other thing that's happened for me, personally, is that my sphere of influence has changed. By that I mean I got asked, for example, a couple of years ago to be the keynote speaker to the Women's Congressional Caucus; these are all the women in Congress, governors, and lieutenant governors in America. I said, "What do you want me to talk about, what topic?" They said, "Whatever you think we need to know to be better legislators." And I thought, "Wow, they want me to tell them about what laws they should be making and what would make a better culture?" Well, that wouldn't have happened if our books hadn't come out and I hadn't become famous. I think I get to play with people at a higher level and have more influence in the world. That's important to me, because my life purpose is inspiring and empowering people to live their highest vision so the world works for everybody, and I get to do that on a much bigger level than when I was just a high school teacher back in Chicago.

Wright

I think one of the powerful components of that book series is that you can read a positive story in just a few minutes, come back and revisit it. I know my daughter, who is thirteen now, has three of the books, and she just reads them interchangeably. Sometimes I'll go into her bedroom and she'll be reading one of them and crying. Other times she'll be laughing, so they really are chicken soup for the soul, aren't they?

Canfield

They really are. In fact, we have four books in the *Teenage Soul* series now and a new one coming out at the end of this year. I was talking to one of my sons—I have a son who's eleven, and he has a twelve-year-old friend who's a girl. We have a new book called *Chicken Soup for the Teenage Soul on Tough Stuff.* It's all about dealing with parents' divorces, teachers who don't understand you, boyfriends who drink and drive, and stuff like that, and I asked her, "Why do you like this book?" (It's our most popular book among teens right now.) And she said, "You know, whenever I'm feeling down I read it, and it makes me cry, and I feel better. Some of the stories make me laugh and some of the stories make me feel more responsible for my life. But, basically, I just feel like I'm not alone."

One of the people that I work with recently said that the books are like a support group between the covers of a book, to hear other peoples' experiences and realize you're not the only one going through something.

Wright

I have been booking speakers for twelve years. I read that you have a speakers bureau with the *Chicken Soup* series authors.

Canfield

Yes, it's called the Souperspeakers Bureau.

Wright

Are those the people who have contributed to your books?

Canfield

Yes.

Wright

That's a great idea.

Canfield

Yes, it's wonderful, and we get a lot of wonderful speakers who are absolutely inspirational and motivational and can deliver a good content. It's nice to know that we're able to do that, to bring messages of hope and inspiration to people.

Wright

Jack, with our *Mission Possible!* talk show and publication, we're trying to encourage people in our audience to be better, to live better, and be more fulfilled by listening to the examples of our guests. Is there anything or anyone in your life that has made a difference for you and helped you to become a better person?

Canfield

Yes, and we could do ten shows just on that. I'm influenced by people all the time. If I were to go way back, I'd have to say one of the key influences in my life was Jesse Jackson when he was still a minister in Chicago. I was teaching in an all-black high school there, and I went to Jesse Jackson's church with a friend one time. What happened for me was that I saw somebody with a vision. This was before Martin Luther King was killed, and Jesse was one of the lieutenants in his organization. I just saw people trying to make the world work better for a certain segment of the population. I was inspired by that kind of visionary belief that it's possible to make change.

Then, later, John F. Kennedy was a hero of mine. I was very much inspired by him. And later, a therapist by the name of Robert Resnick, whom I had for two years, taught me a little formula called E+R=O that stands for Events+Response=Outcome. He said, "If you don't like your outcomes, quit blaming the events and start changing your responses." One of his favorite phrases was, "If the grass on the other side of the fence looks greener, start watering your own lawn more." I think it helped me get off any kind of self-pity I might have had because I had parents who were alcoholics and that whole number. It's very easy to blame them for your life not working. They weren't real successful or rich, but I was surrounded by people who were, and I felt like, "What if I'd had parents like they had? I could have been a lot better." He just got me off that whole notion and made me realize the hand you were dealt is the hand you've got to play, and you've got to take responsibility for who you are and quit complaining and blaming others and get on with your life. That was a turning point for me.

I'd say the last person who really affected me big time was a guy named W. Clement Stone, who was a self-made multimillionaire in Chicago. He taught me that success is not a four-letter word; it's nothing to be ashamed of, and you ought to go for it. He said, "The best thing you can do for the poor is not be one of them. Be a model for what it is to live a successful life." So I learned from him the principles of success, and that's what I've been teaching now for the last, almost thirty years.

Wright

He was the entrepreneur in the insurance industry, wasn't he?

Canfield

He was. He had Combined Insurance, and when I worked for him he was worth six hundred million dollars—and that was before the dot-com millionaires came along in Silicon Valley. He just knew more about success. He was a good friend of Napoleon Hill, who wrote *Think and Grow Rich,* and he was a fabulous mentor. I really learned a lot from him.

Wright

I miss some of the men that I listened to when I was a young salesman coming up, and he was one of them. Napoleon Hill was another one, and Dr. Peale—all of their writings made me who I am today. I'm glad that I got that opportunity.

Canfield

One speaker whose name you probably will remember, Charlie Tremendous Jones, says, "Who we are is a result of the books we read and the people we hang out with." I think that's so true, and that's why I tell people, "If you want to have high self-esteem, hang out with people with high self-esteem. If you want to be more spiritual, hang out with spiritual people." We're always telling our children, "Don't hang out with those kids." The reason we don't want them to is that we know how influential people are with each other. I think we need to give ourselves the same advice. Who are we hanging out with? We can hang out with them in books, cassette tapes, CDs, radio shows like yours, and in person.

Wright

One of my favorites was a fellow named Bill Gove from Florida. I talked with him about three or four years ago, and he's retired now. His mind is still as quick as it ever was. I thought he was one of the greatest speakers I had ever heard.

Canfield

He had one of the greatest voices too.

Wright

What do you think makes up a great mentor? In other words, are there characteristics that mentors seem to have in common?

Canfield

I think there are two obvious ones. One, I think they have to have the time to do it, and two, the willingness to do it. And then, three, I think they need to be someone who is doing something you want to do. W. Clement Stone used to tell me, "If you want to be rich, hang out with rich people. Watch what they do, eat what they eat, dress the way they dress. Try it on." It wasn't, like, give up your authentic self, but it was that they probably have habits that you don't have. Study them; study the people who are already like you. I always ask salespeople in an organization, "Who are the top two or three in your organization?" I tell them to start taking them out to lunch and dinner and for a drink and find out what they do. Ask them, "What's your secret?" Nine times out of ten they'll be willing to tell you. It goes back to what we said earlier about asking. I'll go into corporations and say, "Who are the top ten people?" They'll tell me, and I'll say, "Did you ever ask them what they do differently from you?" They say, "No." "Why not?" "Well they might not want to tell me." "How do you know? Did you ever ask them? All they can do is say no. You'll be no worse off than you are now." So I think with mentors you just look at people who seem to be living the life you want to live, achieving the results you want to achieve. We tell them in our book that when you approach a mentor they're probably busy and successful and so they haven't got a lot of time. Just say, "Can I talk to you for ten minutes every month?" If I know it's only going to be ten minutes, I'll probably say yes. The neat thing is, if I like you, I'll always give you more than ten minutes, but that ten minutes gets me in the door.

Wright

When you consider the choices that you've made down through the years, has faith played an important role in your life?

Canfield

Yes, totally. I believe deeply that I was born with a purpose, a mission. As I told you earlier, it's to inspire and empower people to live their highest vision in such a way that the whole world works for everybody. I always had faith that I was doing God's work and that I was being supported by God and spiritual energies that are available to me. I've always taken risks. I've made the commitment of my time and my resources to do the things that I feel driven to do. For example, when it became clear I was supposed to put together a book of stories and didn't have a title, which eventually became *Chicken Soup for the Soul,* half of my staff said, "You're crazy. You can't make any money. Books don't sell that well. That's a dumb title. You need to be out there doing speeches. Quit writing. Let's do more marketing for your talks." And here we are, over sixty-eight million copies of our books sold now. But I felt divinely inspired. It was like divine obsession. I trusted that if I did what I was hearing in my inner voices in my heart—I call it not my will, but thy will—then the resources would be there to support me. It's the old thing: if you'll jump, we'll build wings on the way down. That's been my belief all along. I believe that I am part of the universal flow of spiritual energy, and so faith in that is very critical to my life and faith in God.

Wright

In the future, are there any more Jack Canfield books authored singularly?

Canfield

Yes, I'm working on two books right now. One's called $E+R=O$, which is that little formula I told you about earlier. I just feel I want to get that out there, because every time I give a speech, when I talk about that, the whole room gets so that you could hear a pin drop; it gets silent. You can tell that people are really getting value. Then I'm going to do a series of books on the principles of success. I've got about a hundred and fifty of them that I've identified over the years. I have a book down the road I want to do called *No More Put-Downs,* which is a book probably aimed mostly at parents, teachers, and managers. There's a culture we have now of put-down humor; whether it's *Married With Children* or *All in the Family,* there's that characteristic of macho put-down humor. There's research now that's showing how bad it is for kids' self-esteem, co-workers, and athletes when the coaches do it, so I want to get that message out there as well.

Wright

It's really not that funny, is it?

Canfield

No, we'll laugh it off because we don't want to look like we're a wimp, but underneath we're hurt. The research now shows that you're better off breaking a child's bones than you are breaking his spirit. A bone will heal much more quickly than his emotional spirit will.

Wright

I remember recently reading a survey where people listed the top five people who had influenced them in their lives. I've tried it on a couple of groups at church and other places. In my case, and also in the survey, it's running that about three out of the top five are always teachers. I wonder if that's going to be the same in the next decade.

Canfield

I think probably, because as children we're at our most formative years. We actually spend more time with our teachers than we do with our parents. Research shows that the average parent interacts verbally with each of their children only about eight and a half minutes a day. Yet at school you're interacting with your teacher for anywhere from six to eight hours, depending on how long your school days is—and coaches, chorus directors, and all that kind of thing. So I think that in almost everybody's life there's been that one teacher who loved you as a human being, not just a subject matter—some person they were supposed to fill full of history and English. And that person believed in you and inspired you. Les Brown is one of the great motivational speakers in the world. If it hadn't been for one teacher who said, "I think you can do more than be in a special ed class; I think you're the one," he'd probably still be cutting grass in the median strip of the highways in Florida instead of being a $35,000-per-talk speaker.

Wright

I had a conversation one time with Les when he was talking about this wonderful teacher that discovered he was dyslexic. Everybody else called him dumb, and one lady just took him under her wing and had him tested. His entire life changed because of her interest in him.

Canfield

I'm on the board of advisors of the Dyslexic Awareness Resource Center here in Santa Barbara. The reason is, I taught high school with a lot of kids who were called at-risk—kids who would end up in gangs and so forth. What we found over and over was that about seventy-eight percent of all kids in the juvenile detention centers in Chicago were kids who had learning disabilities—primarily dyslexia, but there were others as well. They were never diagnosed, and they weren't doing well in school, so they'd drop out. As soon as you drop out of school, you become subject to the influence of gangs and other kinds of criminal and drug-linked activities. If they had just diagnosed these kids earlier—and there are a lot of really good programs that can teach dyslexics to read and so forth—then we'd get rid of half of the juvenile crime in America.

Wright

My wife is a teacher, and she brings home stories that are heartbreaking, about parents not being as concerned about their children as they used to be, or at least not as helpful as they used to be. Did you find that to be a problem when you were teaching?

Canfield

It depends on what kind of district you're in. If it's a poor district, the parents could be drugged out, on alcohol, not available, basically. If you're in a really high-rent district, the parents might not be available because they're both working, coming home tired, they're jet-setters, they're working late at the office because they're workaholics. Sometimes it just legitimately takes two paychecks to pay the rent anymore. I find that the majority of parents care, but often they don't know what to do. They don't know how to discipline their children. They don't know how to help them with their homework. They're not passing on skills that they never got. Unfortunately, the trend tends to be like a chain letter. The people with the least amount of skills tend to have the most number of children. The other thing is, you get crack babies. In Los Angeles, one out of every ten babies born is a crack baby.

Wright

That's unbelievable!

Canfield

Yes, and another statistic is fifty percent of kids, by the time they're twelve years old, have started experimenting with alcohol. I see a lot of that in the Bible Belt. It's not the big city, urban designer drugs, but you get a lot of alcoholism. Another thing you get, unfortunately, is a lot of—let's call it familial violence, a lot of kids getting beat up and hit, parents who drink and then explode. And as we talked about earlier, child abuse and sexual abuse. You see a lot of that.

Wright

Most people are fascinated by these TV shows about being a survivor. What has been the greatest comeback that you have made from adversity in your career or in your life?

Canfield

You know, it's funny; I don't think I've had a lot of major failures and setbacks where I had to start over. My life's been on kind of an intentional curve. But I do have a lot of challenges. Mark and I are always setting goals that challenge us, and we always say, "The purpose of setting a really big goal is not so that you can achieve it so much, but it's who you become in the process of achieving it." A friend of mine, Jim Rose, says, "You want to set goals big enough so that in the process of achieving them you become someone worth being." I think that to be a millionaire is nice, but so what? People make money, they lose it. People get the big houses, they burn down, or Silicon Valley goes belly up and all of a sudden they don't have a big house anymore. But who you became in the process of learning how to do that can never be taken away from you. So what we do is, we constantly put big challenges in front of us.

We have a book coming out in a month called *Chicken Soup for the Teacher's Soul.* You'll have to be sure to get a copy for your wife. I was a teacher, and I was a teacher trainer for years. But in the last seven years, because of the success of the *Chicken Soup* books, I haven't been in the education world that much, so I've got to go out and relearn how to market to that world. I met with a superintendent of schools. I met with a guy named Jason Dorsey, who's one of the number one consultants in the world in that area. I found out who has the best-selling book in that area. I sat down with his wife for a day and talked about her marketing approaches.

So I believe that if you face any kind of adversity, whether you lose your job, your husband dies, you get divorced, you're in an accident like Christopher Reeves and become paralyzed, or whatever, you simply do what you have to do. You find out who's already handled this and how they did it. Then you find out either from their book or from their tape or by talking to them or interviewing them, and you get the support you need to get through it. Whether it's a counselor in your church or you go on a retreat or you read the Bible, you do something that gives you the support you need to get to the other end, and you have to know what the end is that you want to have. Do you want to be remarried? Do you just want to have a job and be a single mom? What is it? If you reach out and ask for support, I think people really like to help other people. They're not always available, because sometimes they're going through it. But there's always someone with a helping hand. Often I think we let our pride get in the way. We let our stubbornness get in the way. We let our belief in how the world should be get in our way instead of dealing with how the world is. When we get that out of that way, then we can start doing that which we need to do to get where we need to go.

Wright

Do you still provide self-esteem resources and training to social workers, welfare recipients, and H&R people? Is it through The Foundation for Self-Esteem?

Canfield

Yes, I have in Culver City (which is part of Los Angeles) a foundation called The Foundation for Self-Esteem. It's run by a man named Larry Price. We've developed a number of programs, one that everyone on welfare in California has to go through, called the GOALS program, and we've been successful in lowering the amount of time people stay in this program for retraining and getting people off the welfare rolls. We've also got that program in San Quentin prison. It's in a number of prerelease programs for prisons. We're now developing a program called Y.E.S., which is Youth Empowerment Seminars, using the same principles. We teach what we call the ten steps to success. It's all the kind of stuff that you and I have been talking about on this show and that are in the book, like the power of focus and so forth. We've made it a video-based program that can be taught to anybody, at any reading level, and get them motivated and excited about life and taking responsibility and doing the things they need to do. It's a good example of what we were just talking about. People on welfare are facing adversity, and it's just a way that shows them what they need to do to get off.

Wright

Are there other states involved in things like that?

Canfield

Yes, we've got our program in thirty-five states, but in most other states it's not a mandatory program like it is in California. We've had over 430,000 people go through this program. We get letters all the time from people saying, "I wish I'd learned this in school." We got a letter from a prisoner the other day saying that if he'd learned these principles before he was eighteen, he wouldn't have had to do what he did that allowed him to go to prison. We had another guy up in Oregon who had read *Chicken Soup for the Soul* that someone had sent him in prison. He said, "If I had read stories like this when I was a kid, or they had been read to me, I wouldn't be here either."

Wright

I was reading some material about you in preparation for this interview. I can remember when I was in junior high school there was a man who was a coach at the school. Most of us really respected him. Of course, I kept up with him all the way through my college days. When I was in my late thirties, I met him one day and I still called him "Coach." It was such a term of endearment and respect. When I was reading the material, it said that you are best described as "an understanding, compelling, empowering and compassionate coach." Is that a title that you're proud of?

Canfield

Yes, I think so. I consider myself a success coach or a life effectiveness coach, not a football coach or a track coach. But as I said earlier, we all need coaches. I could not have played football in high school or track and basketball if I hadn't had a coach to teach me what to do. Unfortunately for the American school system, someone did a research study recently that showed that less than ten percent of the American high schools ever teach anything about goal setting, how to create a balanced life, communication skills, conflict management skills, or how to resolve problems. I always tell people that no one got divorced because they didn't memorize the seven causes of the Civil War or the five exports of Brazil. The reason we get divorced is that we don't have the basic life skills we need to either choose correctly as a partner or to manage conflicts.

Conflicts come up and people just start pulling away from each other and don't share their feelings. There's an emotional and social education that we never get, and, unfortunately, people have to go out and avail themselves of that education through books, seminars, tapes, and by listening to shows like yours to make up for what should have been taught to us in school. I will tell you that most of the people who are listening to this show are not using the trigonometry and calculus they learned in high school. But they are needing to know how to talk to their kids, how to deal with someone when they're angry, how to develop a good habit when you've got a bad one in its place. I always wished there had been a class in high school called Education of the Self, and that you'd have to study "self" science as well as physical science. Maybe someday we'll have that.

Wright

I can remember being in a room of about three or four hundred people one time, and most of them, I assume, were college graduates. The speaker on the platform asked the question, "How many of you, either in grades 1 through 12 or in college, have walked through a door where the title of the class was Decision Making?" Not one person could hold their hand up. He made the same point that you're making. He went on to say that not only are we not taught to make decisions, the people who love us most protect us from making decisions. Those things are important.

Canfield

Think about money management. The average American will have anywhere from a million to two million dollars go through their hands in a lifetime. That's if you're only making $25,000 to $50,000 a year. If you're making $100,000 a year, you can multiply that by four.

So what happens is that most of us have never had any training in school or college about how to manage our finances, how to plan for retirement. The big secret that all the really successful people know is that from the age of about twenty or twenty-five, if you put away one-tenth of your income every month, by the time you're sixty-three you'll have a million dollars in a stock market account. But most of us start out when we're about fifty, then we'd have to live to be a hundred to have that, so it's a little late. But it's a crime that we don't teach these things like decision making. We make decisions all day long; and a lot of the big ones, like who to marry, what job to take, what church to go to, we're not getting much guidance on.

Wright

If you could have a platform and tell our audience something that you feel would help or encourage them, what would you say?

Canfield

I'd say, number one, believe in yourself, and believe in your dreams, and trust your feelings. I think too many people are trained like, when they're little kids and they're mad at their daddy, they're told, "You're not mad at your daddy." They go, "Gee, I thought I was." Or you say, "That's going to hurt," and the doctor says, "No, it's not," and then he gives you the shot and it hurts. He says, "See, that didn't hurt, did it?" You start not to trust yourself. Or you say to your mom, "Are you upset?" and your mom says, "No," when she really is. So you stop learning to trust your perception. I tell the story over and over: there are hundreds of people I've met who've come from upper-class families where they make big incomes, and the dad's a doctor, and the kid wants to be a mechanic and work in an auto shop because that's what he loves. The family says, "That's beneath us. You can't to that." So the kid ends up being an anesthesiologist killing three people because he's not paying attention. What he really wants to do is tinker with cars. I tell people you've got to trust your own feelings, your own motivations, what turns you on, what you want to do, what makes you feel good, and quit worrying about what other people say, think, or want for you. Decide what you want for yourself, and then do what you need to do to go about getting it. It takes work. I always tell people that I read a book a week, minimum, and at the end of the year I've read fifty-two books. We're talking about professional books, books on self-help, finances, psychology, parenting, and so forth. At the end of ten years you've read five hundred and twenty books. That puts you in the top one percent of people knowing stuff in this country. But most people are spending their time watching TV.

W. Clement Stone told me when I went to work for him, "I want you to cut out one hour a day of TV." I said, "Okay, what do I do with it?" He said, "Read." He told me what kind of stuff to read. He said, "At the end of a year you'll have spent 365 hours reading. Divide that by a forty-hour work week and that's nine and a half weeks of education every year." I thought, "Wow, that's two months." It's like going back to summer school. As a result of that, I have close to eight thousand books in my library. The reason I'm on your show instead of someone else is that people like me and Jim Roane and Les Brown and you read a lot. We listen to tapes and we go to those seminars. That's why we're the people with the information. I always say that your raise becomes effective when you do. You'll become more effective as you gain more skills, more insight, and more knowledge.

Wright

Jack, I have watched your career for over a decade, and your accomplishments are just outstanding. But your humanitarian efforts are really what impress me. I think that you're doing great things, not only in California but all over the country.

Canfield

It's true. In addition to all of the work we do, we have all of our books. We pick one to three charities, and we've given away over six million dollars in the last eight years, along with our publisher who matches every penny we give away. We've planted over a million trees in Yosemite National Park. We've bought hundreds of thousands of cataract operations in Third World countries. We've contributed to the Red Cross, the Humane Society, and on it goes. It feels like a real blessing to be able to make that kind of a contribution in the world.

Wright

Well, we are out of time. I could talk to you all afternoon.

Canfield

Thank you. It was great talking to you as well.

Wright

Today we have been talking to Jack Canfield, the founder and co-creator of the *Chicken Soup for the Soul* book series, which currently has thirty-five titles, and I'll have to update this. It was fifty-three million; how many has it been now, Jack?

Canfield

We're almost up to seventy-eight million. We have a book coming out in just a couple of weeks called *Chicken Soup for the Soul of America*. It's all stories that grew out of September 11th, and it's a real healing book for our nation. I would encourage your listeners to get themselves a copy and share it with their families.

Wright

I will stand in line to get one of those. Thank you so much being on *Mission Possible!*

Jack Canfield
Self-Esteem Seminars
P.O. Box 30880
Santa Barbara, CA 93130
(805) 563-2935, ext. 20
www.jackcanfield.com

Chapter 4

Dr. Rick Bommelje

Dr. Rick Bommelje is a leading authority in the development of leadership listening skills. He is a faculty member in the Department of Organizational Communication at Rollins College in Florida and also serves as a leadership and listening coach to a wide variety of organizations. During the past twenty years, Rick has worked with thousands of professionals in their pursuit of success and significance.

The Interview

David Wright (Wright)

Dr. Rick Bommelje has over twenty-five years of professional experience in leadership, supervision, management, and adult education. Rick is an Associate Professor in the Department of Organizational Communication at Rollins College in Winter Park, Florida. He's also the president of a professional development and educational firm, The Leadership and Listening Institute, that specializes in the development of people's leadership, listening, self-leadership, and teamwork skills. Additionally, he is a leadership and listening coach who helps people one-on-one in their pursuit of success and significance. His practical experience is complimented by a master's degree in management and a doctorate in administration and supervision. Rick has studied teamwork process at the National Training Laboratory Institute for Applied Behavioral Science and has also completed professional development work in leadership and adult education at Harvard University. Rick, welcome to *Mission Possible!*

Rick Bommelje (Bommelje)

Thank you, David. I'm delighted to be with you.

Wright

Rick, you talk a lot about leadership coaching. I was interested, after reading some of the things that you sent me, to learn the four steps you offer as a leadership coach: listen, endorse, advise, challenge. Tell us what you mean.

Bommelje

These four steps are essential in the coaching process. A coach is someone who shows you how to do or master something, whether it be reaching an important goal or making a difficult professional or personal change. Over the years, coaching has evolved into an integrated success technology. It consists of a well-defined system of specialized knowledge, concepts, and strategies. A coach does not just recommend; a coach is actively involved in the client's progress. So both coach and client are committed to making things happen. Clients hire a coach because they want additional structure, inspiration and wisdom—and because they want to be challenged.

One of the most effective and efficient ways to challenge clients is to make requests of them, that is, to ask them directly to do one of three things: one, to start to do something; two, to stop doing something; and three, to change what they are doing.

Wright

Would that also apply in sports coaching? Are you familiar with those kinds of coaches?

Bommelje

Sure, there is indeed a parallel with sports coaching.

Wright

The listening part?

Bommelje

Most definitely. In fact, the really effective coaches are listeners . . . and I'm thinking about the great former UCLA coach John Wooden. He built championship basketball teams year after year, and his teams set records that even today are unmatched. He has written a couple of books that reveal some of his winning strategies. Coach Wooden was a master listener. So the first step in the coaching process is listening. Listening is the most powerful skill that a coach can master.

The second step is to try to get a sense of where people would like to go and then endorse and encourage their journey. It's also about helping the client clarify the difference between a possible opportunity versus a pipe dream.

Then we come to the next step, which is to advise. In many cases, people already have the answers inside themselves. They just need a sounding board to be able to crystallize their ideas into an action plan.

The final step is to challenge the client to follow through on what they say they're going to do and then hold them accountable to it.

Wright

Is the endorsement phase like an agreement phase? I can remember I used to have several salespeople working for me, and each week we would set our goals. They would set their goals, and, basically, my acceptance of what they told me seemed to be a quasi-endorsement.

Bommelje

Yes. In fact, a practical definition of commitment that I like to use with clients is this formula: commitment equals desire plus evidence. We're trying to get the client to develop a measurable piece of evidence that could be produced if they took action.

Wright

Several years ago when I was heading a sales company and goal setting—if a salesman came in and told me he was going to sell two units that week, and I agreed with it, then if he had sold two by Tuesday, he could take the rest of the week off as far as I was concerned, because I had, in fact, agreed with it and endorsed it.

Bommelje

That's a good example of fulfilling a commitment—and producing the evidence.

Wright

I read in one of your leadership articles that you stated research confirms that seventy percent of what we hear is ignored, misunderstood, or forgotten. That depressed me. Is it that high?

Bommelje

Actually, it's approximately seventy-five percent. David, I'm sure that you have come across situations in which listening errors were just rampant in business organizations. These errors have specific costs attached to them. The costs can be measured in terms of loss of money, damaged relationships, low morale, and an endless stream of ineffectiveness that can bring down an organization or a leader.

Wright

I remember listening to several people down through the years, even back as far as the early seventies, and it seems like it hasn't changed. They were either repeating what they had heard or they were repeating the original surveys. These pointed to the fact that no matter what you say nor how eloquently you say it, if you don't use visual aids—if it's just a verbal communication—at the end of the sixteenth day the person will forget all but two percent.

Bommelje

That sounds pretty accurate. In fact the research over the years shows that visual aids in a presentation help to reinforce the understanding and retention of a message. As we explore the listening process, it's such a complex behavior that is frequently taken for granted in life. Many people assume that they listen effectively when, in fact, if you put them to the test, they realize that there are opportunities for development. Then they begin to realize, "Gee, maybe this is an area that I can grow in." I know that was the case for me.

Wright

You know, management is really a tough job. I sympathize, or at least empathize, with some managers, but then there are others who are doing things unethically. We read in the paper every day where managers who are making five, six hundred thousand to millions of dollars a year are taking advantage of their job. Do you really believe that most organizations are over-managed and under-led?

Bommelje

I certainly believe that many of the managers in organizations unfortunately do over-manage rather than focus on their ability to lead. That has adverse impacts as well. Leadership is such a dynamic, electric, magnetic word. The real challenge is for people to recognize that leadership is relational and not positional. It's not about the title. Leadership is something that can be developed at any level within an organization. Especially today, with mergers and downsizing and all kinds of dramatic changes happening in organizations, we need more and more leadership to help organizations move forward. I think that's why you see volumes being written on leadership, because it certainly is something that is a highly visible topic.

Wright

I was talking to one celebrity recently, and he was probably joking or just giving me a line, but he said, "Leadership is finding a parade and getting in front of it." I started thinking that all of the great leaders that I've ever known were filled with vision, and they always walked the way they envisioned it. You could get behind their parade all right, but they sure didn't find a parade. They introduced the parade.

Bommelje

Yes. I also think that it's possible for an effective leader to lead the parade from behind. In fact Lao Tzu years ago said, "To lead the people, walk behind them." I think he was really pointing to a very pivotal way of viewing leadership, focusing on two words—servant leadership. To lead the people, we serve them. That, in some way, is counter to what some folks believe leadership is all about: "Follow me; I am your leader. I will take you to the most appropriate place." Whereas if we can get people to see that they have tremendous potential within themselve—and as a leader my total role is to help you get to where you want to go—interesting things start to happen.

Wright

Many years ago Paul Meyer, who led the goal-setting charge in the early seventies and all the way through the next couple of decades, had a lot to say about leadership. One day he told me that leadership could never be delegated from above; it had to be earned from the people being led. The people let you know whether or not you're a leader.

Bommelje

That's terrific. I have a definition that I use for leadership, which is "guiding people to positive places that they have never been before." Adding to the definition, there are five components: discovery, enthusiasm, resourcefulness, resilience, and contributing to the good of society.

Wright

That's great. When you talk about a situational leader, you refer to organized common sense. What is that?

Bommelje

It's actually organized common practice. We hear the phrase, "Oh, that's just common sense," when some people refer to the "soft skill areas." I believe to a degree it is; however, you can have common sense but not common practice. In other words, "To know and not to do is not to know at all." So situational leadership, which has been a model that has been around for decades, is a way of listening, analyzing where people are within their development stage, and giving them the appropriate leadership style to get them to the next level—diagnosis first, prescription second, just like in the medical profession.

Wright

That would take a lot of your first stage—listening.

Bommelje

Listening is the key to leadership success. That's really what propelled me into a personal search for developing my own listening ability. I can see how it's interwoven in every aspect of life, whether it be professionally or personally.

Wright

Someone told me many years ago that leadership was self-leadership applied to others. I noticed that you talk and write a lot about the topic. Could you tell us what you mean by self-leadership?

Bommelje

Self-leadership is guiding yourself to positive places that you have never been before. It is the first level of leadership. How can we effectively lead other people if we can't effectively lead ourselves? In my opinion, the beginning step of self-leadership is clarifying our personal purpose.

Wright

You mean asking the question, What am I doing here?

Bommelje

Or, Why am I here? Not just, Why am I in my job? Why am I doing this project? But, Why am I on this earth? Once we come up with that answer, I believe every decision that we make from that point forward is either an "on-purpose" or an "off- purpose" decision. If we're off purpose, we can then make the adjustments to get back on.

Wright

When you teach corporations the principles of team building, how do you define the difference between groups and teams?

Bommelje

I encourage people to think about "team" as Napoleon Hill did years ago in his classic *Think and Grow Rich,* in terms of the words "mastermind alliance." A mastermind alliance is built of two or more people working actively together in perfect harmony toward a common definite object. They're committed to a common purpose, they're committed to shared values, they have performance goals, and they've got a working approach. The other key, David, is that in a team, the members are holding themselves mutually accountable to each other. A group consists of two or more people who think they are grouped together for administrative purposes only. The individuals work independently and sometimes at cross-purposes with others.

Wright

That's interesting. Rick, with our *Mission Possible!* talk show and book, we're trying to encourage people in our audience to be better, live better, and be more fulfilled by listening to the examples of our guests. Is there anything or anyone in your life who has made a difference for you and helped you to be a better person?

Bommelje

Without a doubt. There's one person who has been the primary influence in my life, and that's my wife, Quin. Quin was born in Thailand in the northeast part of the country. She has limited formal education but has earned a Ph.D. in wisdom over the years. I have seen more leadership and courage come from her on a consistent basis over the past three decades than I have from some military officers, governmental officials, and corporate executives. She has impacted my life tremendously and has enabled me to grow far beyond what I ever dreamed I was capable of.

Wright

Yesterday was Valentine's Day. I hope you appropriately thanked her!

Bommelje

This was a very special Valentine's Day for us—our thirtieth! One of Quin's favorite sayings, which I have adopted, is, "When things are going good, work harder."

Wright

That is great advice. A lot of sports coaches have told me down through the years that they try to get their players to work on their strengths, not their weaknesses.

Bommelje

We could easily get into a comfort zone which can limit our ongoing growth.

Wright

What do you think makes up a great mentor? In other words, are there characteristics that mentors seem to have in common?

Bommelje

I believe that a mentor is one who is a great listener, is accessible, a sharer of knowledge, a sharer of experience, one who gives freely, and one who in many regards could play the role of a coach. I have a mentor in my life, a dear gentleman who is seventy years old. We have breakfast together once a week. Just to be able to bounce ideas off of him, both professionally and personally, has been a tremendous boost to me. We've had this relationship for over six years.

Wright

That's great.

People are fascinated these days with the new TV shows about being a survivor. What has been the greatest comeback you have made from adversity in your career or in your life?

Bommelje

Well, we've all gone through the fire and, in many cases, many fires. For me, I would say that the greatest comeback has been the realization that I had some serious defects in my ability to listen with—and to—other people. I have been on a fifteen-year quest to upgrade my listening behavior. This began in 1987 when I was guiding a team of fourteen professionals. We were a good team, but not a great team. There were team issues and conflicts that were creating costs. We had missed project deadline dates, lost money, and had tensions between team members. In my mind, I was blaming some of my team members for their lack of initiative and drive. That was getting me absolutely nowhere. What I eventually realized was that it was not my team members; I was the one holding my team back, and that was because of my communication deficiencies. I did a little bit more thinking and realized that I was not listening effectively. From that point forward, I started a journey towards learning as much about my listening as I possibly could, and it continues to this moment. This journey has taken me to fascinating places. For example, I met the father of listening, Dr. Ralph Nichols, who began seriously researching the listening dynamic in the 1940s. I met the gentleman who introduced listening to corporate America, Dr. Lyman Steil, who was instrumental in developing the Sperry Corporation's listening process that gained worldwide acclaim. These listening pioneers were very sharing, warm, and caring leaders, and they gave me wonderful information. I learn primarily through two ways; one is by doing, and the other is by teaching. I brought this information back and started implementing it with my team; I also added it to leadership seminars that I was guiding. The next thing I knew, I delivered about fifteen minutes on listening, and the leader participants seemed to be very hungry for it. That expanded into thirty minutes.

And then, in 1989, the chairmen of the Rollins College Communication Department learned that I was doing some teaching in the area of listening, and he invited me to teach a course at Rollins exclusively on listening. I was comfortable with thirty minutes, but now I was being challenged to develop forty hours worth of dynamic information on listening. Realizing that this stretch opportunity would be a terrific chance to continue my own learning, I accepted the challenge and since that time have been blessed to be able to learn with thousands of professionals throughout the country.

Wright

When you consider the choices that you've made down through the years, has faith played an important role in your life?

Bommelje

Yes. Faith in my God has been the anchor of my personal foundation. I had earlier mentioned my wife, Quin. We met in 1971 when I was stationed in Thailand in the U.S. Army. After I was discharged from the military, Quin joined me in the U.S. and we were married. Quin was a Buddhist when she came to join me in America. Over a number of years, she made the decision to convert from Buddhism to becoming a Christian. As I watched her grow in her faith, I realized that there was something very special happening. For a number of years, I had been searching for what I was calling a need for peace of mind. I realized that the quest for peace of mind was actually the need to have a relationship with Jesus. Through observing her Christ-like actions, Quin led me to know Christ. I am also proud to say that our son, Mark, also has a relationship with Christ.

Wright

That would be a great topic for ministers. Is it rare that Buddhists convert to Christianity?

Bommelje

It is quite unusual.

Wright

If you could have a platform and tell our audience something that you feel would help or encourage them, what would you say to them?

Bommelje

I have a granddaughter, Em, who is five years old, and she has become my master teacher. For example, she taught me how to play again. If you can believe it, David, over the years I forgot how to play.

One day Em was visiting us at our home, and I was working on a computer project. She was sitting next to me and was drawing. I only see her once or twice a month because she lives in another city, so I stopped what I was doing and just watched her immersed in her artwork. All of a sudden—and I think she was about two years old at the time—she looked at me and we made eye contact. In one of her teaching moments, it felt like she telepathically transmitted a powerful message through my eyes into my brain without saying a word. Basically the message was this: "Papoo (that's what she calls me), there are two dimensions of time—'now' and 'not now'! Em is in the 'now', at least at this point in her life. But as she continues to grow older, she's going to lose that. She will begin spending, like many of us do, a lot of her time in the future and a lot of her time in the past, and she's going to miss the moment."

A couple of days later, I was responding to an e-mail message. Before I sent off my response, thinking about Em's wisdom, I wrote three words in my reply: "Make today count." I had an occasion, a few minutes later, to respond to another e-mail, and I sent it with "Make today count." These three words have become my motto. So if there is one piece of advice that I would give to anyone, especially after what happened on 9/11, it is to "Make today count."

Wright

This has been a fast thirty minutes. We have been talking today to Dr. Rick Bommelje, who has over twenty-five years of professional experience in leadership, supervision, management, and adult education. He is an associate professor at Rollins College in Winter Park, Florida, and is also a leadership and listening coach, guiding organizations and individuals toward professional and personal success and significance. Dr. Bommelje, I really appreciate your being a guest on *Mission Possible!* today. Thank you so much.

Bommelje

Thank you, David. It's been a privilege . . . and I challenge you to ***make today count!***

Wright

Thank you. I will do that.

Dr. Rick Bommelje
8530 Amber Oak Dr.
Orlando, FL 32817
(407) 679-7280
E-mail: rbommelje@rollins.edu
www.listencoach.com

Chapter 5

Janet Luongo

Janet Luongo gives speeches and seminars for organizations that want to develop leaders with the vision, creativity and skills to thrive in a topsy-turvy world. Overcoming a youthful crisis to become V.P. of The Discovery Museum and president of the NY chapter of the National Speakers Association, she has turned those organizations around. Janet's vision of creative leadership was broadcast by Sky Radio on 30,000 flights on American and Northwest Airlines in 2002. She brings humor and creativity to clients and sponsors that include Yale-New Haven Health Systems, Bristol Myers, General Electric and Deloitte & Touche.

The Interview

David Wright (Wright)

Today we are talking to Janet Luongo of Norwalk, Connecticut, a multifaceted artist, writer, professional speaker, educator, and curator whose work has been seen and heard in galleries and lecture halls all over the world. Janet grew up in Queens, New York.

She graduated magna cum laude from Adelphi University and received her master's degree in education from CUNY. She is included in numerous Who's Who lists for her accomplishments in the arts and education. She has been a teacher at the International School of Geneva in Switzerland and in the United States. As a speaker, Janet's most requested topics include Creative and Innovative Thinking, Team Building, Leadership, and Cultural Diversity. Janet Luongo, welcome to *Mission Possible!*

Janet Luongo (Luongo)

Thank you.

Wright

Janet, I read an article that you wrote for a women's publication, titled "Women, Money and Art Today." You pointed to a UN study in 1985 that revealed women make up fifty-one percent of the population, do ninety percent of the work, and earn ten percent of the income. Is this still true in the arts?

Luongo

I'm afraid that in the arts there is still quite a gender gap. The latest statistics I have are from the Gorilla Girls West in 1999. They counted up the number of female artists in standard history, art history textbooks used in college. It's unbelievable, really. They found that from 1962 to 1995 Janson's *History of Art* was one hundred percent male, so that's not giving a very good impression to the female students in the class. They did finally update it in 1995 and included thirty-eight women, but that's still about 98.7% male.

We still have that problem. One of the things I work on, that I'm committed to, is having the voices of people, whether they're women or anyone else, be heard so they can develop their expression.

Wright

I know you're a painter. Thank you for sending me some of your work; I really did enjoy it. I was really surprised at those statistics. I know it's bad, but it's not that bad in other fields. Do men paint better than women?

Luongo

No, I don't think so. I think that fifty percent of the artists are women, or more than fifty percent. It is getting better, but we're still not fully represented in the galleries. Art exhibits are mounted with fewer than ten percent women, so there's still a lot we need to do—and not only in art. Let me share this story with you. I just talked to one of my students at Sacred Heart University. (I teach communications there.) She's taking a business course as well, and she told me that her male teacher actually said—and this is now— that woman's place is in the kitchen, and women should not be managers. I thought he must have been joking, but she said that he really believed that men would not work for a female boss. This is right now, this month, so it's discouraging. But in my experience, things are improving.

Wright

I was interested in a reply from Judy Chicago, an artist in Santa Fe, to a letter you wrote to her in 1992, where she said, in part, "Our (women's) destiny as artists is linked to the destiny of our gender, so joining together is the only way we can survive or advance."

Do you feel that the same is true in most occupations?

Luongo

I think that we all like to get together with people we feel like we belong with, whether that's your family, a tribe, a professional group, an ethnic group, or by gender, where we feel totally comfortable and we can get support and be strengthened. My goal is that after we get that strength to not stay in that little group but to go out into the mainstream and make our contributions to everyone. Too many people, I think, just stay within their own enclave where they feel secure. But I think periodically you do need to go back and be with people who give you the most strength.

Wright

I really thought that, at least in the United States, women were being treated more equally than at any time in the past. But in the arts it doesn't seem to be true, does it?

Luongo

There's still prejudice. The art history books, as I said, still don't have much women's art, but we are working on it. I've worked with the Women's Caucus for Art for ten years, a non-profit organization that specializes in trying to get the voices of women and people of color to be heard more. I started a chapter in Connecticut, and we're working on getting catalogs. We've had forums in museums, and we are getting the word out.

Wright

Only a creative artist would name her company Open Minds Open Doors. Tell us a little about your company. Do you specialize in training?

Luongo

Yes, I do, and I'm glad that you mentioned the name. I thought about that for a long time, and I thought, If I'm a creative person, I don't want to have a dull name, like Creative Enterprises, that anyone can have. Let me have a name that's visual and different so it shows what I really stand for. When I got right down to it, that's what I wanted to teach people—how to open their minds. I believe strongly, as we were talking about, in opportunity for all, so open doors was the next part of it. But yes, I specialize in training—speaking and training—and setting up the business and working in it is certainly a challenge, because entrepreneurs have to do just about everything. We have to be total people. I've always wanted to be independent, and the style of being an entrepreneur suits me a lot. I love it!

Wright

A lady who called me last week had seen all about my company on the Internet. There's a picture of me there that has "president" under it. She said, "Oh my, I'm talking to the president." And I said, "Yes, and I just finished cleaning the toilet!"

Luongo

Right. We're the president, secretary, accountant, treasurer, everything—and yes, the janitor.

Wright

The topic that fascinated me as I read one of your presentations was "The Creative Process." I have always been interested in creativity and innovation. Can you give us a layman's view of the process?

Luongo

Absolutely, that's what I do. I speak to people who don't necessarily think of themselves as creative people. The process is similar across fields. Studies have been done, and the one I'm referring to is by Career Track. They have a wonderful CD called "Creativity and Innovation." There and in other texts it's been shown that people who are creative have the same process whether they're scientists, writers, artists, or entrepreneurs. It doesn't matter. Business people certainly have to be creative, as we know. The process is similar. It starts, usually, with a question or a problem that you want to solve, and then you have to start to prepare. The first stage is preparation, so you have to gather data, do research, work (and work hard) at that stage.

The second stage is called incubation. At that stage we stop. We incubate like a little baby that's not quite ready to be born. You have to just rest and sometimes take a nap and go to sleep. We say, "Let's sleep on it." You have to let the idea gel. You have to let all the facts you've accumulated integrate and come to something in your own mind. Then, when we least expect it, often when we wake up or when we're in the shower or sitting in the train or car, we suddenly get what we call the inspiration—we hope—and that's the third thing. That's the "Aha!" Then, after that, you can't just say, "Oh, I have the best idea for a book!" You have to actually write the book. So that's the fourth stage, verification, where you actually do the work, or, if you're a scientist, you go back to the lab and work it out. You make sure it's replicable and can be published and put out in the world. That goes for anybody; it's the same basic process.

Wright

Janet, are there common traits that creative people seem to have?

Luongo

Yes, that's another thing that we've found out lately in the research. It comes down to actually two. There were many more traits that people thought made someone creative, but it's really only two. It has very little to do with your being the most talented; it has to do with your own belief that you're creative. Within that belief, if you believe you're a creative person, you usually have curiosity about the things that you specialize in. You have the confidence to do something about it (to follow it up, to speak about it). You have the courage to stand up for the idea and to keep trying it, even though you may be failing. And you stick to it—constancy, persistence. You can have the best idea in the world; but if you're not going to really work at it and get it to the stage where it can help others, then you haven't done much. That all comes under the one trait of belief that you're creative.

The second trait is creative introspection. It's been found that most creative people, again, in any field, understand the process of creativity. They will spend some time reading about other creative people. They'll spend time in solitude, and they have some understanding of their own originality. They're basically introspective in some way. It doesn't mean they can't be extroverted in other ways; but regarding creativity, most people have some time that they spend in introspection.

Wright

I've noticed my own creativity seems to be fleeting. I used to write a lot of choral music for churches. Sometimes I would get a great idea. I would hear everything from the flutes to the violins; I'd hear it all while driving down the interstate. I would think to myself that it's a great tune, and when I get home I'll write it down. It never happened. I should have simply pulled over right that minute and at least jotted down the melodic line, because by the time I got home it was lost forever.

Luongo

Wow, I think that what you need is one of those recorders that you can keep in your car and maybe hum the tune!

Wright

With our *Mission Possible!* talk show and book, we are trying to encourage people in our audience to be better, live better and be more fulfilled by listening to the examples of our guests. Is there anything or anyone in your life that has made a difference for you and helped you to be a better person?

Luongo

Oh sure, there are so many. I always come back to this one person in the third grade. She was my teacher, and she was African-American, one of the only African-Americans in our school in Queens, New York. I thought she was one of the most beautiful people in the world because she was so kind. She was very patriotic. She would sing to us "America" in the school assembly, and she would just touch my heart with the power of her voice. The thing that she told us was that nothing is impossible. I remember her saying that: "Nothing is impossible." She told us that people in the past believed that human beings could never fly, and now we fly in airplanes. So she said that you can do anything; let yourself dream. She was so supportive of me. She told my mother that I could do very well in any subject I chose, but I would have to make that choice someday. She said the best way to choose would be to find the thing that you love. She was very wise, and she gave me a whole view of myself and of the world that was very open and encouraging and gave me a lot of confidence.

Wright

I wondered, after reading in your bio where you've lived in places other than the United States, which place that you have lived has influenced your life the most?

Luongo

Of course, starting in New York City, which is very special and diverse. I got used to the diversity there; when my husband and I were married for two years, we decided to live in Europe. We went to Geneva, Switzerland. We were planning to go for only two years, but we liked it so much we stayed for eight. It certainly had a huge impact on my life. He worked as an English teacher, and I eventually taught at the school as well, in art, and was actually the chair for one year. I began to enjoy the diversity. I was able to learn to speak French fluently. We traveled all over, from Scotland and Spain to Egypt and Israel. We saw the Berlin Wall before it came down, which was quite something historically. I also spent most of my time writing and painting. I wrote my first novel there. After we were there four years, I created my greatest masterpiece, and that was our son, David. We really had a great time in Switzerland. It was a very special place to raise a small child. It was so safe and a beautiful, natural environment. He had a ball. He went with us to Vienna on the overnight train. We visited relatives in Hungary. He sat in double-decker buses in London. He skied in the Alps and swam in the Mediterranean. That's not so bad for a four-year-old!

Wright

What was your most important experience there?

Luongo

I was very happy to be able to paint and exhibit. I did exhibit in several galleries in the area. I was invited to exhibit and had a one-person show at an established gallery in Geneva—Gallery Motte. I saw this exhibit as being the culmination of a lot of the work I was doing in Europe after seven years in painting—all the studies and all the work I had seen. It took a great deal of work. The woman who ran the gallery, Madam Motte, was very well connected, and she had me interviewed by a national paper before the exhibit. My hopes were very high, because she had a lot of patrons. Since I had sold work at every other gallery, I thought surely I would sell work at her gallery.

So I invested in materials, frames, and beautifully printed invitations. Then I had to work for a whole year to put the thirty paintings together. My husband was very supportive. He loves my art, and he would work with me so that we would have time to take care of our son and work, yet still have a few hours in the studio to do my painting. I was pretty busy and didn't have much time to think of too much else, like politics, money, finances, the economy.

When the time rolled around in April—I had picked April because it's the beginning of the new spring season, and people (I was hoping) would come down from the avenues, stroll, and want to buy some art. But I was in for a few surprises, David. The week right before the exhibit opened, President Reagan ordered the bombing of Libya. Libya is close to Europe, and it made Europeans very nervous. It reminded me of the Cuban Missile Crisis, if you remember that. We were all afraid that this incident would escalate; nobody really knew what would happen. It started some anti-American feelings, unfortunately, in Geneva. Markets were down at that time; exchange rates were not good. Then on the evening of the exhibit, April 22, there was a snowstorm. April—and this is not in the mountains, this is in the valley, and this does not usually happen. So I was just shocked. It was driving snow, and I was totally discouraged. And sure enough, Madam Motte's old patrons did not come out in the storm. My friends were there, but I didn't sell one work. After that, for one whole week, it rained. At the end of the week was one of the worst international disasters ever. That was when the nuclear power plant in Chernobyl blew up. What else could go wrong? Here was my best opportunity, and then one thing right after the other. What it really showed me is how you can't do what I did, which was to isolate myself in my studio and not pay attention to everything else. Everything else was impacting on me—politics, wars, markets, weather. It certainly made me also count my blessings.

Wright

You've mentioned Jim, your husband, being with you in almost everything you've done. Did I read that you wrote a play that he directed? I loved the title. It was something like "My Father Who Art in Florida." Is that right?

Luongo

Right, it's called "Our Father Who Art in Florida." Yes, we work together well. That was a fund-raiser for the Women's Caucus, and it was a play about my family. Even though it discussed some heavy issues, it was really a comedy, so the audience was laughing at the right places. It was quite a wonderful experience.

Wright

You're also the author of the story (and I think you have it on CD and video) "How I Got My Paintings to Paris Despite Stupid Bureaucrats." You can surely come up with some titles! Maybe you'll title my next book.

Luongo

They tell me titles are very important. Yes, that was a lot of fun. That was another adventure, how I got my paintings past the regulations and the Swiss border guards. They can be quite efficient and formidable. They almost blocked me from having an exhibit of several of my works in Paris. After a lifetime of hoping—Paris was the center of the art world—they were telling me no, I couldn't get my paintings through. The story is about all the obstacles I had to face on the journey and how I overcame each one of them because I really wanted to go there. Nothing was going to stop me.

Wright

A lot of people in the United States are glued to their TV sets watching these new programs about being a survivor. What's the greatest adversity that you have come back from in your career or in your life?

Luongo

There have been a few things that have set me back, but one of the biggest was something that happened thirty-five years ago, and, David, I have never spoken about this in public. But I think after thirty-five years it might be time to go public with it because it was a very important thing. I was seventeen when I graduated from high school. I was in an accelerated program and very young for graduating. Just at that time my parents had a divorce. The home really fell apart at that time. There had been a lot of anxiety and alcoholism up until that point, but we kind of held together. Just at that point, when I graduated, everything fell apart. I went to live with my sister who was younger than me, sixteen. The two of us had an apartment in New York at that age; she was still in high school. It wasn't easy for us. The following year I left home completely and went to art school. My father did try to help me with the tuition there. I had a boyfriend who one night came over with mescaline. Even though this was the sixties and drugs were all around me, I was not particularly interested in getting high. I made a very poor choice and agreed and said, "Okay, I'll just take a little bit of this." The problem was a little bit was even worse, because I didn't just say, "Okay, now I'm going to trip." I didn't even know what would happen. I didn't think it would affect me, and so when I started to hallucinate it seemed real. It really was a terrible experience. I went on what they call a bad trip and didn't even know it.

It took two years for me to really come back from that, to get back on track. So that was quite a setback. But I did come back and got back to school, got back to college, and finally got my master's. You learn that you're a human being, you make mistakes, and you have to forgive yourself and you have to forgive other people. You can't carry that around. I learned how to empathize with other people's suffering and setbacks. Even though these things seem so terrible, they do build your character. I figured if I could get through that, I could get through just about anything.

Wright

What helped you make the comeback?

Luongo

As I said, forgiving people and myself. Then I met the man who became my husband and I got my first job teaching. Art also helped me a great deal. I know the power of creativity. We mentioned the play already. Writing things like that—writing it down, seeing the characters up on the stage and being able to manipulate them and laugh at them—really helped. My first novel was about those hard times in the sixties, so art is really a very powerful way of developing yourself and getting back to your inner heart.

Wright

What do you consider to be your best accomplishments?

Luongo

Well, let's see. I'm very happy that I have such a wonderful husband. We've been together now twenty-seven years. One of the things that my father said when I was in a very low period was that you can't really go back to school or maybe you won't ever be able to find a husband and have a normal life. I look back at those times and see that I was able to find a wonderful person to love, and together we've had a beautiful son. We're very proud that we've been able to give him a home that is stable and loving, and we were able to invest in his education. He's turned out to be such a wonderful young man.

Wright

When you consider the choices you have made down through the years, has faith played an important role in your life?

Luongo

Yes, I have a great faith in the potential of the human being. I have a faith that there is a higher power who guides each one of us. I don't know why I believe that, so I guess that's faith. We have no real evidence, so that's faith; I believe in that. My father had moved us into the Unitarian Universalist faith when I was a child, and I still practice that today with my husband and son. The basis of that religion is free-thinking and tolerance and a belief in the interconnectedness of all things. Those beliefs are really the fountainhead of my mission for my business too. That's what I teach—openmindedness.

Wright

A friend told me many, many years ago what I consider to be the best definition of faith I've ever heard. He said, "You have to walk as far as you can in the light, and take one more step into the darkness"—light meaning understanding and knowledge, darkness meaning ignorance. I believe that, whether you're talking about faith in yourself or faith in a higher being. I think it fits either way.

If you could have a platform and tell our audience something you feel would help or encourage them, what would you say?

Luongo

I think I would tell people to be themselves and to take time out to listen to the small, quiet voice inside of them, to take action, to create spaces where they can develop their creativity. I would ask them to open their minds to alternative points of view and not to put themselves down, not to talk against themselves or anyone else, because that has a negative effect. Develop a dream; picture the place you want to go, and create a plan that will get you there. We're always growing; therefore, we never reach the final destination while we're alive, but at least we can move on to the next station.

Wright

That would be good advice. Anything else?

Luongo

I love Maya Angelou. She had some very tough times as a youth herself, and she says, "You can't use up creativity. The more you use, the more you have."

Wright

That's great. Do you know the time is up? It's been thirty minutes. I've learned so much, and I really appreciate you being with us.

Luongo

I really loved talking with you, David.

Wright

Today we have been talking to Janet Luongo of Norwalk, Connecticut. She's an artist, writer, professional speaker, educator, and we have learned from her today. We really appreciate her being with us on *Mission Possible!* Thank you so much, Janet.

Luongo

Thank you, David.

Janet Luongo

Open Minds Open Doors, LLC

(203) 846-2642

Toll Free: (877) 307-4486

Fax: (203) 846-0339

E-mail: janet@openminds-opendoors.com

www.openminds-opendoors.com

Chapter 6

Brian Tracy

Brian Tracy is one of America's leading authorities on the development of human potential and personal effectiveness. He's a dynamic and entertaining speaker with a wonderful ability to inform and inspire audiences toward peak performance and high levels of achievement.

The Interview

David Wright (Wright)

Many years ago, Brian Tracy started off on a lifelong search for the secrets of success in life and business. He studied, researched, traveled, worked, and taught for more than thirty years. In 1981, he began to share his discoveries in talks and seminars, and eventually in books and audio- and video-based courses. The greatest secret of success, he learned, is this: "There are no secrets of success." There are, instead, timeless truths and principles that have to be rediscovered, relearned, and practiced by each person. Brian's gift is synthesis, the ability to take large numbers of ideas from many sources and combine them into highly practical, enjoyable, and immediately usable forms that people can take and apply quickly to improve their life and work. Brian has brought together the best ideas, methods, and techniques from thousands of books, hundreds of courses, and from experience working with individuals and organizations of every kind in the U.S., Canada and worldwide. Today, I have asked Brian to discuss his latest book, *Victory! Applying the Military Principals of Strategy for Success in Business and Personal Life.* Brian Tracy, welcome to *Mission Possible!*

Brian Tracy (Tracy)

Thank you, David. It's a pleasure to be here.

Wright

Let's talk about your new book, *Victory! Applying the Military Principals of Strategy for Success in Business and Personal Life.* By the way, it is refreshing to hear someone say something good about the successes of the military. Why do you think the military is so successful?

Tracy

Well, the military is based on very serious thought. The American military is the most respected institution in America. Most people in America really respect the military, because it keeps America free. People who join the military give up most of their lives for twenty to thirty years and sacrifice to be prepared to guard our freedoms. And if you ask around the world what it is that America stands for, they'll say that it stands for individual freedom, liberty, democracy—freedom and opportunity that is only secured in a challenging and dangerous world by our military.

Now the other thing is, the people in our military are not perfect, because there is no institution made up of human beings that is perfect. There are no perfect people. The cost of mistakes in military terms is death; therefore, people in the military are extraordinarily serious about what they do. They are constantly looking for ways to do what they do better and better and better, to reduce the likelihood of losing a single person.

We in America place extraordinary value on individual human life. That is why you will see millions of dollars spent to save a life, whether an accident victim or Siamese twins from South America, because that's part of our culture. The military has that same culture. I was just reading today about the Predator drone plane used in places such as the no-fly zone in Iraq. These pilotless planes fly back and forth, constantly picking up information from the ground. They can also fire remote-controlled weapons. The planes cost two to three million dollars each and get shot down on a regular basis. However, the military is willing to invest hundreds of millions of dollars to develop these planes and even lose a plane at a cost of two to three million dollars if it will save a pilot, because pilots are so precious, because human life is so precious. So in the military, everything is done right down to the tiniest detail, because it's the tiniest details that cost people's lives. That is why the military is so successful, because they are so meticulous about planning, and they are careful.

A salesperson can go out and make a call; if it doesn't work, fine; you make another call. A professional soldier can go out on an operation, and if it's not successful they're dead, and maybe everybody else is dead as well. There is no margin for error in the military; that's why they do it so well. That's why the military principles of strategy that we talk about in *Victory!* are so incredibly important, because a person who really understands those principals and strategies sees how to do things vastly better, with far lower probability of failure, than the average person.

Wright

In the promotion of *Victory!* you affirm that it is very important to set clear, attainable goals and objectives. Does that theme carry out through all of your presentations and all of your books?

Tracy

Yes, over and over again. You can't hit a target that you can't see; you can't get into your car unless you know where you are going. More people spend more time planning a picnic than they spend planning their careers. I'll give you an example: A very successful woman, who is in her fifties now, wrote down a plan when she was in a university. Her plan was that for the first ten years, she would work for a Fortune 500 corporation and really learn the business and learn how to function at high levels. For the second ten years of her career, she talked about getting married and having children, at the same time working for a medium-size company and helping to grow it into a very successful company. For the third ten years, between the ages of forty and fifty, she would start her own company, based on her knowledge of both businesses, and she would build that into a successful company. Her last ten years she would be the chief executive officer of a major corporation and retire financially independent at the age of sixty. At age fifty-eight she would have hit every single target. People would say, "Boy, you sure are lucky." No, from the time she was seventeen she was absolutely crystal clear what she was going to do with her career and what she was going to do with her life, and she hit all of her targets.

Wright

In a time where companies, both large and small, take a look at their competition and basically try to copy everything they do, it was really interesting to read in *Victory!* that you suggest taking vigorous offensive action to get the best results. What do you mean by vigorous offensive action?

Tracy

Well, see, that's another thing. When you come back to talking about probabilities—and this is really important—you see successful people try more things. And if you wanted to just end the interview right now and ask, "What piece of advice would you give to our listeners?" I would say, "Try more things." The reason is that if you try more things, the probability is that you will hit your target. For example, here's an analogy that I use. Imagine that you go into a room and there is a dartboard against the far wall. Now imagine that you are drunk, and you have never played darts before. The room is not very bright, and you can barely see the bull's-eye. You are standing a long way from the board, but you have an endless supply of darts, so you pick up the darts and just keep throwing them at the target over there on the other side of the room, even though you are not a good dart thrower and you're not even well-coordinated. If you kept throwing darts over and over again, what would you eventually hit?

Wright

Pretty soon you would get a bull's-eye.

Tracy

Yes, eventually you would hit a bull's-eye. The odds are that as you keep throwing the darts, even if you are not that well-educated, even if don't come from a wealthy family, or you don't have a Harvard education, if you just keep throwing darts you will get a little better each time you throw. It's called the cybernetic mechanism of self-correction in the brain—each time you try something, you get a little bit smarter at it. So over time, if you keep throwing, you must eventually hit a bull's-eye. In other words, you must eventually find the right way to do the things that you need to do to become a millionaire. That's the secret of success. That's why people come here from so many countries. They come here with one idea in mind: "I can try anything I want; I can go anywhere, because there are no limitations. I have so much freedom; and if I keep doing this, then, by God, I will eventually hit a bull's-eye." And they do, and everybody says, "Boy, you sure were lucky."

Now imagine another scenario. First, you are thoroughly trained at throwing darts; in other words, you have practiced; you have developed skills and expertise in your field. You are constantly upgrading your knowledge; you practice all the time. Second, you are completely prepared; you're cold sober, fresh, fit, alert, with high energy. Third, the room is very bright around the dartboard. You go in, and you know how to throw darts. This time, how long would it take you to hit the bull's-eye? The obvious answer is, you will hit a bull's-eye far faster than if you had all those negative conditions.

So what I am saying is that you can dramatically increase the speed at which you hit your bull's-eye. The first person that I described—drunk, unprepared, in a darkened room, and so on— may take twenty or twenty-five years. But if you are thoroughly prepared, constantly upgrading your skills; if you are very clear about your targets; if you have everything you need at hand and your target is clear, you could hit a bull's-eye in five years rather than twenty. That's the different in success in life.

Wright

In reading your books and watching your presentations on video, one of the common threads that we see is creativity. I'm glad that in the promotional material of *Victory!* you state that you need to apply innovative solutions to overcome obstacles. The word "innovative" grabbed me. I guess you are really concerned with *how* people solve problems, rather than just solving them.

Tracy

The question about trying more things—vigorous action means you will cover more ground. What I say to people, especially in business, is the more things you do, the more experience you get. The more experience you get, the smarter you get. The smarter you get, the better results you get. The better results you get, the less time it takes you to get the same results. And it's such a simple thing. You will find in my books *Create Your Own Future* and *Victory!* that there is one characteristic of all successful people— they are *action-oriented;* they move fast, they move quickly, they don't waste time. They're moving ahead, trying more things, but they are always in motion; and the faster you move, the more energy you have; the faster you move, the more in control you feel; the faster you are, the more positive, the more motivated you are. We are talking about a direct relationship between vigorous action and success.

Wright

Well, the military certainly is a team sport, and you talk about building peak performance teams for maximum results. My question would be, How do individuals in corporations build peak performance teams in this culture?

Tracy

One of the things we teach is the importance of selecting people carefully. Really successful companies spend an enormous amount of time at the front end on selection. They look for people who are really, really good in terms of what they are looking for. They interview very carefully; they interview several people and interview them several times. They do careful background checks. They are as careful in selecting people as a person might be in getting married. Again, in the military, before people are promoted, they go through a rigorous process. In large corporations, before people are promoted, their performance is very, very carefully evaluated by the people around them. They make sure they are the right people to be promoted at that time.

Wright

My favorite point in the *Victory!* book is when you say, "Amaze your competitors with surprise and speed." I have done that several times in business, and it does work like a charm.

Tracy

Yes, it does. One of the things we teach over and over again is that there is a direct relationship between speed and perceived value. When you do things fast for people, they consider you to be better; they consider your products to be better; they consider your service to be better. They actually consider them to be of higher value. Therefore, if you do things really, really fast, then you overcome an enormous amount of resistance. People wonder, Is this a good decision? Is it worth the money? Am I going in the right direction? Is there a better way to do it? And when you do things fast, you sort of blast that out of their minds.

Wright

You talk about moving quickly to seize opportunities. I have found that it is difficult. When I ask people about opportunities, it's difficult to find out what they think an opportunity is. Many think opportunities are high-risk, although I've never found it that way myself. What do you mean by moving quickly to seize opportunity?

Tracy

There are many cases were a person has an idea, and they think it's a good idea and that they should do something about it. They think, "I am going to do something about that, but I really can't do it this week, so I will wait till after the month ends," and so on. By the time they do move on the opportunity, it's too late; somebody's already seized it.

One of the military examples that we use is the Battle of Gettysburg. Now the Battle of Gettysburg is considered the high-water mark of the Confederacy. After the Battle of Gettysburg, the Confederacy won additional battles at Chattanooga and other places, but they eventually lost the war. The high-water mark of Gettysburg was a little hill at one end of the battlefield called Little Round Top. As the battle began, Little Round Top was empty. Colonel Joshua Chamberlain of the Union Army saw that this could be the pivotal point of the battlefield. He went up there and looked at it, and he immediately rushed troops to fortify the hill. Meanwhile, the Confederates saw that Little Round Top could be key to the battle as well, so they, too, rushed the hill and an enormous battle took place. It was really the essence of the Battle of Gettysburg. The victor who took that height controlled the battlefield. Eventually, the Union troops, who were almost lost, controlled Little Round Top and won the battle, and the Civil War was over in about a year and a half. That was the turning point.

So what would have happened if Chamberlain had said, "Wait till after lunch, and then I'll move some men up to Little Round Top"? The Confederates would have seized Little Round Top, would have controlled the battlefield, and would have won the Battle of Gettysburg. It was a matter of moving very, very fast. There are three days that were considered, forty years later, to be the reason for the loss of the Battle of Gettysburg. In charge of the troops on the Confederate right flank was General James Longstreet. Lee told him to move his army forward as quickly as possible the next day, but to use his own judgment. Longstreet didn't agree with Lee's plan, so he kept his troops sitting there most of the next day. And they say it was Lee's failure to move forward in the second day and seize Little Round Top that cost the Confederacy the battle and eventually the war. It was just his failure to move forward; and forty years later, when Longstreet appeared at a reunion of Confederate veterans in 1901 or 1904, he was booed. They felt that he had cost them the war—his failure to move forward the second day. If you read every single account of the Battle of Gettysburg, they talk about Longstreet's failure to move forward the second day, quickly, to seize the opportunity that was right in front of them.

Wright

In your book, you tell your readers to get the ideas and information they need to succeed. Where can individuals get these ideas?

Tracy

We are living in an ocean of ideas. It's so easy. The very first thing you do is pick a subject you want to major in, and you go to somebody who is good at it. You ask what you should read in this field, and you go down to the bookstore and look at the books. Any book that gets into paperback obviously sold well in hardcover. Read the table of contents. Make sure the writer has experience in an area that you want to be good at. Buy the book and read it. People ask, "How can I be sure it is the right book?" You can't be sure; stop trying to be sure.

When I go to the bookstore, I buy three or four books and bring them home and read them. I may only find one chapter of the book that's helpful, but that chapter may save me a year of hard work. The fact is your life is precious. A book costs twenty or thirty dollars. How much is your life worth? How much do you earn per hour? A person who earns fifty thousand dollars a year earns twenty-five dollars an hour. A person who wants to earn a hundred thousand dollars a year earns fifty dollars an hour. Now, if a book costs you ten or twenty dollars but it can save you a year of hard work, then that's the cheapest thing you have bought in your whole life. And what if you bought fifty books and paid twenty dollars apiece for them—that's a thousand dollars worth of books—and out of that you only got one idea that saved you a year of hard work? You've got a fifty times payoff. So the rule is, you cannot read too much, and you cannot prepare too thoroughly.

Wright

In the last several months I have recommended your book *Get Paid More and Promoted Faster* to more people. I have a lot of friends in their fifties and sixties who have lost their jobs to layoffs and all kinds of transfers of ownership. When I talked to you last, the current economy had a sixty-five percent jump in layoffs. In the last few months before I talked to you, every one of them reported that your book really did help them. They saw some things a little bit clearer. It was a great book.

How do you turn setbacks and difficulties to your advantage? I know what that means, but what's the process?

Tracy

You look into every setback and problem and find the seed of an equal or greater advantage or benefit. It's a basic rule. You will find that all successful people look into their problems for lessons they can learn and for things they can turn to their advantage. In fact, one of the best attitudes you can possibly have is to say that you know every problem that is sent to you is sent to help you. So my job is to just simply look into it and ask, "What can help me in this situation?" And surprise, surprise! You will find something that can help you. You will find lessons you can learn; you will find something you can do more of, or less of; you can find something that will give you an insight that will set you in a different direction, and so on.

Wright

I am curious. What are your personal plans for the next few years? I know you have written a lot in the past, and you are a terrific writer. Your cassette programs are wonderful. What do you have planned for the next few years?

Tracy

I intend to write four books a year. I already have my four books scheduled for publication in 2003. I have published four books this year. I have my four books planned for 2004. So we are right on track. Aside from speaking and consulting with nonprofits, my goal is to produce four books a year on four different subjects, all of which have practical application to help people become more successful.

Wright

Well, I really want to thank you for being with us today on *Mission Possible!* It's always fascinating to hear the things that you say. I know I have been a Brian Tracy fan for many, many years, and I really appreciate you being with us today.

Tracy

Thank you. You have a wonderful day, and I hope our listeners will go out and get *Focal Point* and/or *Victory!* You can get them from any bookstore or Amazon.com. They are fabulous books, filled with good ideas that will save you years of hard work.

Wright

I have already figured out that those last two books are a better buy with Amazon.com, so you should go to your computer and buy these books as soon as possible.

We have been talking today to Brian Tracy, whose life and career truly make one of the best rags-to-riches stories. Brian didn't graduate from high school, and his first job was washing dishes. He lost job after job—washing cars, pumping gas, stacking lumber, you name it. He was homeless, living in his car. Finally, he got into sales, then sales management. Later, he sold investments, developed real estate, imported and distributed Japanese automobiles, and got a master's degree in business administration. Ultimately, he became the COO of a $265 million dollar development company.

Brian Tracy, you are quite a person. Thank you so much for being with us today.

Tracy

You are very welcome, David. You have a great day!

Brian Tracy International
462 Stevens Ave., Suite 202
Solana Beach, CA 92075
(858) 481-2977
www.briantracy.com

Chapter 7

Allison Blankenship

Allison Blankenship develops leaders through tactful communication skills, self-management strategies, and life balance solutions. As founder of the Enrichment Center of Southwest Florida, Inc., Allison is recognized as a motivation expert who delivers easy-to-apply ideas on achieving success through attitudes and actions.

The Interview

David E. Wright (Wright)

Today we're talking with Allison Blankenship, Executive Director of the Enrichment Center of Southwest Florida, Inc., and the 2001-2002 president of the Florida Speakers Association. Allison is recognized as a leader in personal development breakthroughs. She presents more than 150 programs a year on communication, leadership, and life balance skills. Some of her clients include Wal-Mart, Bank of America, GE Client Services, and Textron Financial.

She received her bachelor of arts degree in Mass Communications from Auburn University and has been selected as an Outstanding Young Woman of America. Allison Blankenship, welcome to *Mission Possible!*

Allison Blankenship (Blankenship)

Thank you, David; it's a pleasure to be here.

Wright

Allison, tell us a little about the Enrichment Center—specifically, what do you do there?

Blankenship

We're a motivation management company based in Naples, Florida. I founded the company in 1996 and was very purposeful in choosing the phrase "motivation management." Throughout my corporate career, I found that most people assume employees are motivated from the outside. What we know is that people are, of course, motivated internally. That's been a great key for me in helping others achieve their personal success. Our focus is twofold. First, we develop people's internal motivation, or attitude. Then we go back and give them the skills they need to take action. That essentially is my business and personal philosophy: *Attitude+Action=Success*™.

Wright

So people are motivated from within by their attitudes—do you mean that they motivate themselves?

Blankenship

Absolutely. There is no such thing as an unmotivated person—everyone thinks they know some, but it's not true. People are either motivated to perform or not to perform. And you can tell by their attitude. That's why time and time again we find that money is a temporary motivator at best. Even some of the highest paid people will walk away from a job because it is just not worth the hassle and aggravation that they perceive. Our mission is to work with individuals to guide them in identifying those internal attitudes that keep them motivated, as well as what demotivates them. Your attitude is the only guaranteed controllable factor in your life. People are surprised to learn that.

Wright

What are some of the barriers you find that keep people from meeting their goals and living their dreams, or companies from being efficient and productive?

Blankenship

It's interesting, David; we find many universal themes out there. Most of these internal demotivators or attitudes (we call them barriers) are rooted in fear. There was a study that came out about two years ago that talked about a condition called the "imposter syndrome." It is estimated that ninety percent of the American public suffers from the imposter syndrome. Essentially, what that means is that people are afraid that others will find out they're not who they think they are. We all have a persona or attitude that we put on, or we act in a certain way because we think we need to, or we think that's what other people like. Quite honestly, none of these acts or actions are who we really are. So you can see where that starts to cause a little bit of internal stress, a bit of internal friction, and eventually that internal attitude becomes external. That's one way companies end up with attitude problems, morale problems, conflict, and infighting.

Wright

Are you talking about low self-image?

Blankenship

Self-image is a part of it. I would put it under the umbrella of confidence. The average person on the street would tell you, "I've got great self-esteem. I'm really confident." Yet if you talk to them, after a few minutes they'll make a comment like, "You know, my boss is really a jerk," or "Nobody really appreciates me," or "Life is so unfair." Those are all barriers, demotivators, negative attitudes, which are all flags of low self-confidence. Did you know that it takes less than seven seconds to change your attitude? Most people are good at creating a positive self-image but don't know what actions to follow through with. Thinking about success is not enough—you have to take action. Hence the *Attitude+Action=Success*™ formula. The challenge comes when people don't know the right actions to take or how to put together a strategic directional plan. They just react, it backfires, so they develop a negative attitude and give up. It really can be a vicious cycle. In our work, we really emphasize understanding our attitudes and choices, then put together an action plan. We call it a personal success contract—the "attitude" with a strategic directional plan, the "action." That way, you've got the motivation and direction to accomplish your goals.

Wright

I've been reading a lot about you. You've got quite an amazing personal story for someone as young as you are. Twice you've overcome extreme medical situations, including invasive cancer, and twice you've been at the height of your career only to see those jobs disappear overnight. What lessons have you learned from that?

Blankenship

Quite a few! I spent the first thirty years of my life fighting adversity and all the obstacles that came my way. That resulted in a lot of frustration. I felt as though life was really just one big struggle, and quite honestly, it had an impact on my personal faith. I hadn't developed my success formula yet and constantly resisted changes in my life. Cancer was actually what changed my attitude about adversity—it is really and truly a part of life. When I changed my attitude to one of "response-ability," instead of trying to find ways to avoid challenge, I became more productive and successful. How you respond or react is what makes the difference. When we respond instead of react, we come from a place of confidence and peace. Reacting is letting those negative thoughts or self-doubts stop you from having what you really want. Whenever I speak to a group or work with a company, I always reinforce that the key to success is to respond, not to react.

Wright

My wife is a six-year cancer survivor. I heard her say something in a meeting the other day with a group of people that I thought she'd never say. She said that whereas she wouldn't want to have cancer again, she wouldn't give a million dollars for the experience. She helps a lot of people now. It's really unbelievable how going through such a tremendous strain on the family, as well as on yourself, and facing possible death, you could come out on the other side and actually help other people.

Blankenship

David, the key is to recognize that cancer occurs not because you're a bad person, but because your body is trying to send you a message. We have to take better care of ourselves. The wonderful, intensively productive lives Americans lead have consequences if we don't stop and take care of ourselves along the way. Cancer has taught me to balance my life with purpose.

Wright

I know you've got fifteen years of experience working for some large, well-respected corporations. In your opinion, what is the worst thing that companies are doing today to lose good employees?

Blankenship

It's the same problem that we've had for years, but it's disguised itself a little bit. I would say that the worst thing we're doing to lose good employees is we're just not communicating properly, or we're not communicating well, especially with face-to-face communications. So many organizations tell me, "We have a communication problem." When I break it down, it's more of an issue where people are not willing to communicate honestly. They're overwhelmed because business has accelerated so much that they don't feel they have time to communicate with each other. We see teams that aren't getting feedback from other teams or from their managers. People feel isolated and frustrated; many become demotivated because no one gets positive feedback, only negative. Then you have all the technology with e-mail and cell phones and checking everything. In my opinion, communication is the biggest crisis in America. It's come up recently, of course, with so many of the corporate scandals, like Enron, where dishonest communication was the bottom line. The facts were not presented truthfully.

I had a similar experience many, many years ago when I worked for Eastern Airlines. I remember the day I was furloughed—that's a fancy word for "laid off"! This was before the company officially went bankrupt, but no one had any idea how desperate the situation really was. I remember walking off of a flight, checking with my flight supervisor, and he said, "You know, Allison, you need to go look at that wall over there." We had a big bulletin board in the employee lounge. I couldn't imagine what was happening—there was a tremendous amount of crying and wailing, so I thought that we'd crashed an airplane. I went over to the wall and there was a huge computer list that read, "The following employees need not report back to work." My name was on that list. I knew then that if this is how the organization communicated its business to employees, then the airline was not going to make it. Two years later it was out of business.

Communication may be the greatest challenge that we have, but helping people communicate through change is a key element to resolving that challenge. The acceleration of change is just huge. David, you were probably at the same conference I was last summer where they talked about how the rate of information is doubling. Global knowledge is increasing every eleven months. They predict that within a year it will be every six months. When I tell people this, they're just overcome. Their eyes glaze over. They don't really know how to manage all that. Their reaction is extreme stress and conflict. I think on top of the communication issue, companies need to work with their employees to help them understand that change is job security. It's not negative; it's positive. Consistent change is what's going to keep us employed for the next ten to fifteen years. Teaching people how to communicate effectively and honestly and then working with them to grasp the change process are probably the best keys to holding good people.

Wright

I remember telling a friend of mine a few weeks ago that I felt that back in the seventies and eighties when I was running large businesses I could read everything that I wanted to and keep up with most of what was going on in my industry. Now I feel like I'm sitting in front of a fire hydrant and the knowledge is coming at me full force and I'm drinking with a straw. I can't even get to all of the magazines.

Blankenship

Therein lies the problem, David. We feel indebted to get to all the information instead of looking at what information is going to be best for me or for our project or for our group. You have to develop the skill that I call rethinking—looking at information in a different way, seeing it as a commodity almost, and not something that has to be absorbed individually. There's going to be so much more information out there as our global knowledge accelerates. We have to find what's right for us.

Wright

I'm a real nut when it comes to creative titles. I was in Las Vegas one time with a red carpet company meeting of about a thousand people. When we registered they had our packet there at the desk. I got my packet and opened it and saw that a fellow named Chris Christianson (this was back about 1983) was doing the keynote the next morning. The title of his speech was "You Can't Lead a Charge Up the Hill If You Think You Look Funny Sitting on a Horse." I was in the front row; I couldn't miss that. I knew it had something to do with self-esteem.

Allison, tell us about your upcoming book, *Real Women Have Chipped Nails: How to Live an Imperfect Life and Love It.*

Blankenship

That's right: *Real Women Have Chipped Nails.* You'll find it at www.chippednails.com. A major portion of my business is working with women on leadership and communication skills. I travel all over the country, and every time I go to a company or attend an association or speak to a group, I ask them to tell me, "What is your biggest obstacle to success?" The answer is always a resounding "Myself!" What I've found is that over seventy percent of the women surveyed have totally unreal expectations of themselves and oftentimes the people around them. I was shocked. I thought the types of things I was hearing had gone out fifteen or twenty years ago—they were very similar to the superwoman theories. Women between twenty-five and fifty-five still put undue pressure on themselves.

Being a reformed perfectionist myself, I wanted to write a book for other women on, basically, how to let go of that craving to control, or the belief that if I do it just right, people will accept me. Yes, those are self-esteem issues, but it's also about being balanced. What I find so interesting is that an alcoholic or a reformed smoker will tell you that not a day goes by where they don't want that drink or that cigarette. The same is true for perfectionists. We have to learn new skills and re-examine what we expect of ourselves and other people. *Attitude+Action=Success*™ is a strong theme, not surprisingly! The book is written in the female perspective, but it certainly applies to men. We're having the best time with the chapter titles. There's one that you'll probably appreciate. It's a story about when I was first married, and it's called "The War of the Tomatoes." My husband ate the only remaining tomato—how dare he?! It's a funny story. Although it's about conflict on the surface, it's also a message for people that we have to fill our own emotional cup. Expecting other people to look out for us is foolish, and that's what leads to unhappiness. You can get a sneak preview of the book at www.chippednails.com.

Wright

You reminded me of a great friend that I had in South Carolina. He's a fourth-generation Presbyterian minister. One Saturday I saw him; the next day, Sunday, we were going to have an open house at the parsonage. I asked him where his wife was and he said, "She's home dusting the rafters in the attic." At least she knew what you were talking about!

With our *Mission Possible!* talk show and book, what we're trying to do is encourage people in our audience to be better, live better, and be more fulfilled by listening to the examples of our guests. Is there anything or anyone in your life that has made a difference for you and helped you to become a better person?

Blankenship

David, I've enjoyed a very full life; and if I had to single out one part of that life, I would probably say that becoming a stepmom has been my proudest accomplishment. I married late in life, and where I'm from in Alabama, getting married at thirty-four is definitely over the hill. We received his-and-her cemetery plots for wedding presents! (Just kidding!) Anyway, my husband has two beautiful children from his first marriage who were very young when we married. And despite the fact that I was very excited to become an instant "mom," we just weren't prepared for it—primarily due to a conflict of values. Unfortunately, I discovered that I didn't necessarily like these kids. They weren't nice people, according to my standards. There was a lot of struggle between my unconditional love for my husband and my very conditional love for his children.

A woman who has been a great impact on my life gave me some incredible advice on that situation. She's my aunt, Imogene Davis. When sharing with her some of the struggles I had with these young kids, her response had a profound effect on my life. She told me that people don't want to be fixed; they just want to be loved. Isn't that the truth? It's allowed me to back off and let them be who they are, and try to teach them the life skills I think are necessary. Because of that (and they're teenagers now), I have two great kids. Whenever that "fix other people" urge surfaces, I remember Imogene's advice to back away and let them be who they are. It's not always easy, but we have an excellent level of respect and value for each other.

Wright

That is a great lesson!

What do you think makes up a great mentor? In other words, are there characteristics that mentors seem to have in common?

Blankenship

I would say that good mentors have probably these three characteristics. First, there has to be mutual respect and trust between the two parties, and second, it needs to be mutually beneficial. Many times we think of mentoring as one way, and that's actually not the case. There needs to be reciprocal benefit for both parties. Third, mentors definitely need to be good listeners, and they need to be good problem solvers. Mentoring is an excellent way for corporations to bridge quite a few generational and skill gaps.

Several years ago when I was still in public relations, I had an incredible experience. I was asked to work on a major project with a woman in our company whom we'll call Joan. Joan was fifty and I was thirty-three. Joan was very much a perfectionist, beyond my wildest dreams, and probably the only person in the whole company that I found difficult to get along with. This was a three-month project with me as the lead. In the beginning, we really struggled until I began mentoring Joan to build the confidence to make her own decisions. I did that by stepping back and observing her for a few days, and then combining what I observed with some personal information that I knew. Every time she would come to me and say, "What should I do?" I would just deflect it right back on her and say, "I don't know, Joan; what do you think? Why don't you research that and tell me what you think?" She would come back a little while later and we would go through this process again and again. David, it took a good two weeks, but by the end of two weeks she developed a trust with me that I would not criticize her and that she could come to me for advice. I watched this fifty-year-old woman blossom in front of my eyes. It was really wonderful.

Wright

You looked at it from the mentor's point of view, then?

Blankenship

Of course! It was an excellent experience in patience for me in learning how to develop people, because I knew that if I could grow her professional skill of making competent decisions, then my job was going to be a lot easier. It was definitely mutually beneficial.

Wright

The statistics seem to point to that fact in so much of what I've read.

On occasion I ask groups of people to list the five people who have made a real impact or a difference in their lives, and out of the top five an average of about three are teachers. I started thinking back in my own life, and boy, there were some great teachers. There was a seventh-grade teacher who treated me with such respect and brought things out of me that I didn't know I had. I'll never forget her.

Blankenship

I just spoke with another professional who, as a young man, was labeled as a youth at risk. He has a wonderful story about a teacher who pulled him aside and said, "Listen, you are not a youth at risk. You are a youth at promise." What a difference that simple attitude shift made for him! That was another example of a teacher being just an incredible catalyst for this young man to take action and be successful.

Wright

When you consider the choices you've made down through the years, has faith played an important role in your life?

Blankenship

Very much so. I think, honestly, David, faith was probably something that I took for granted. When I married, my stepchildren had not been to church on a regular basis. That was something that I wanted very much to make a part of our family life. I remember one night tucking my little son into bed, and I said, "Let's say your prayers." He looked at me just as honestly as he could and asked, "Why do you pray?" I was at a loss for words—I'd never had to think about that! That was eight years ago, and it has really led me to think about why we do have faith in our lives. It's opened the doors to a journey of a wonderful spiritual relationship beyond prayer, beyond faith, to actually living in the spirit. This is what I call the spirit versus your ego. It's living in a self-focused manner that is certainly different from self-centered. I think all of us have a spirit, an essential part of ourselves that is divine love and divine inspiration. When we lose that connection with our spirit, that's when the ego comes in with negative attitudes and stress. Interestingly enough, when I experienced cancer, I reacted by being angry with God. I had been very faithful and very devout, and I didn't feel as though I "deserved" this to happen. That's a very common reaction to adversity. Of course, that experience led me once again to the revelation that bad things don't happen to good people on purpose and that attitude determines our outcome. How we respond and what we do with the opportunities that life and God give us makes all the difference in the world. My personal belief is that in every awful situation there is a silver lining.

Consider the ramifications of 9/11. I was scheduled to present several stress management and life balance programs the following week. The clients wanted to go ahead with them even though I was a bit hesitant. People attending the programs amazed me. They stopped and really examined their lives and focused on the purpose of their being instead of just going through the routine. People made sincere commitments to what was most important to them, rather than what was most important to others. It was extremely empowering. So as tragic and horrendous as that event was, I see it as a spiritual awakening for America.

Wright

You know, most people are fascinated by the new TV shows about being a survivor. Other than the cancer, what has been the greatest comeback you have made from adversity in your career or in your life?

Blankenship

Actually, David, I think it was probably before the cancer. Earlier I told you the story about being employed by Eastern

Airlines. When I walked off that airplane and had no job, I was stunned. It was a total surprise to everyone involved. I was in my early twenties and didn't have any money in the bank, and to make a long story short, I ended up in line for food stamps. Here is a college-educated person who has had a fairly privileged life, and I thought, "Why is this happening to me? I don't deserve this." David, let's be honest—no one deserves to be there.

Luckily for me, I recognized my "stinkin' thinkin'" for what it was and got out of the line. I decided I hadn't given it my all yet. I wasn't ready to go on assistance until I was absolutely destitute. I signed up with an employment agency and they gave me a great job that paid one hundred dollars a day—that was a lot of money back then. But I had to wear a costume. That should have been the first clue. I walked into the costume store and I thought, "Okay, how bad could it be, really?" I'm thinking a Garfield or some big fuzzy suit. Well, she put me in this southern belle costume that was peach colored with a hoop skirt the size of Kansas. That wouldn't have been so bad except I was assigned to work at the World of Concrete show. You can imagine the "elite" clientele that attends the World of Concrete show! For five days I was a southern belle at the World of Concrete, and every single person that walked by me would look at me and point and say, "Look over thar; it's a Georgia Peach!" I must have heard that at least five hundred times a day! Trust me, resembling the official state fruit was bad enough, but hearing the same comment over and over was like Chinese water torture.

Wright

That should have made you irate. Weren't you raised in Alabama?

Blankenship

Absolutely! Southern is southern, though. That experience formed the basis of my *Attitude+Action=Success™* formula. It really taught me the value of planning, and from that point on I've had a personal plan in place. I recovered and went on to reach one of the highest accolades in my career, which was becoming a regional director for a five-star hotel company. It was also a great confidence builder to know that I can overcome life's obstacles and low points.

Wright

I was reading with interest a lot about you before this interview, and I couldn't help but be taken aback that you appeared on *NBC Nightly News,* you were selected as an Outstanding Young Woman of America, and seven years later you qualified for food stamps. That's kind of high and low, isn't it?

Blankenship

And it was that way for the first thirty years—a lot of roller coaster rides!

Wright

Has it leveled out for you now?

Blankenship

Absolutely, by just learning to enjoy and appreciate what I have, even the adversity that comes along. I'm just thankful I know that there will be a great lesson in it for me and hopefully for the people around me. Understanding that has really evened out those bumps.

Wright

How about the family; is it smooth going now?

Blankenship

With two teenagers it's been the usual struggle. You probably remember being a fifteen-year-old boy, right?

Wright

I remember raising a fifteen-year-old girl and a fifteen-year-old boy who are now forty and thirty-nine, and now I'm raising a thirteen-year-old.

Blankenship

Bless you! Truthfully, I've really enjoyed the teenage years despite the bumps. You know what's so funny, Dave, in becoming a parent? I was a manager for a long time before I was a parent, but I never realized the parallels between managing people and raising children. That's been a great resource. We have a good time.

Wright

If you could have a platform and tell our audience what you feel would help or encourage them, what would you say to them?

Blankenship

I'd share my personal three secrets of success. Number one, remember it's not the cards you're dealt in life, it's how well you play the game. We need to learn how to respond to both challenges and opportunities instead of reacting. Attitude is the first step in the success equation! I would also say, number two, that success and fulfillment come from within you. I have seen many people be unhappy for a long time because they expect others to take care of their needs or make them happy or make them successful. I really believe that when you act responsibly for your life's success then your path becomes clear and you can follow that. That's the taking action part of the formula.

And I would say, number three, we really need to spend time connecting with that higher self. I just believe that no one will ever love you like you love yourself, so my message to men and women is you'd better get good at it. You'd better appreciate who you are and love you for you, because in the end there's no guarantee. I really believe that when we face the great Creator we'd better have a good reason on why we should be let in.

Wright

I had a mentor tell me once, "You are the only one that you will never leave nor never lose." When you think about that, in my life a lot of people that I have loved are gone now.

You say that about fifty percent of your business is with women. Do you see a changing in the corporate world today? Are women more respected now? I know with all the laws and everything the wages are getting better, but are they really as respected as they should be?

Blankenship

I think in some areas yes and in others no. David, I don't know if there's ever going to be a completely level playing field, because I don't think that's ever occurred in the history of mankind, between men and men, or men and women. Where I see women's talents are primarily being utilized is in being great team leaders, excellent consensus builders. And many women are excellent communicators. Smart companies are really capitalizing on those strengths. Where I still see some stereotypes or prejudice is usually in salary and benefits differences—the scales are still uneven. However, I will add that oftentimes I see people really play into the stereotypes and use them as excuses not to take action or be responsible for their own success. I think in many ways we've come a long way as far as the female workforce, but there's a little bit further to go.

Wright

Well, we are out of time. This has been a fast thirty minutes; I could talk to you all day.

Today we have been talking to Allison Blankenship, Executive Director of the Enrichment Center of Southwest Florida, Inc. She is also the 2001-2002 president of the Florida Speakers Association.

We really do appreciate you being with us today, Allison. Thank you so much for being on *Mission Possible!*

Blankenship

Thank you, David; it's my pleasure. If anyone would like more information on what we've covered, please visit www.chippednails.com.

Allison Blankenship, Executive Director
Enrichment Center of Southwest Florida, Inc.
4880 Sycamore Drive
Naples, FL 34119
(239) 455-7899
Fax: (239) 455-6969
E-mail: allison@enrichmentcenter.com
www.allisonspeaks.com
www.chippednails.com

Chapter 8

Paula A. Sassi, C.G.

Paula A. Sassi, C.G. is a certified graphologist, who has worked professionally in the field of handwriting analysis since 1980. Owner of Handwriting Consultants International, Paula provides workshops and consulting services on personnel selection, team building and behavioral profiling for a diverse group of clients throughout the United States. She is a professionally published author and has been featured on local and national television and radio shows, analyzing the handwritings of the famous and infamous.

The Interview

David Wright (Wright)

Today we are talking to Paula Sassi, who has worked professionally in the field of handwriting analysis since 1980. Owner and director of her own corporation, Paula serves a diverse group of clients in the area of personnel selection, behavioral profiling, and compatibility analysis. Top businesses and corporations seek her services for help in hiring and promoting personnel as well as in conflict resolution. Author of *Better Handwriting in 30 Days,* Paula has been featured on television and radio broadcasts where she analyzed the handwritings of famous and infamous individuals. She has co-authored professional courses in handwriting analysis which are offered through the Academy of Handwriting Sciences. Paula Sassi, welcome to *Mission Possible!*

Paula Sassi (Sassi)

Thank you.

Wright

Paula, what a unique occupation. How did you get started in this fascinating field?

Sassi

Simply by taking a free class in adult education. Then I went on to private lessons and got certified through a national organization. After that, I felt I needed more education, so I put myself through college and got a degree in psychology.

Wright

Adult education—that's something. Were you fascinated with handwriting or were you just picking courses?

Sassi

I was looking through the adult education brochure, and handwriting analysis looked interesting, so I just showed up one night, and it totally changed my life.

Wright

Isn't that something. How long have you been in the handwriting business?

Sassi

After studying for five years, I opened my own business in 1980 and incorporated in 1997, so altogether I've been practicing in the field of handwriting analysis for twenty-seven years.

Wright

Is there a lot of information that people can get if they want to study handwriting analysis? Or how do you dig up the information?

Sassi

One way is to come to me. I offer a correspondence course in handwriting analysis.

Wright

Oh, is that right?

Sassi

Yes.

Wright

So anyone can simply start learning? If they wanted to go into it as an occupation, they could start learning it on what, the Internet?

Sassi

Actually, we have a correspondence course, so we can either do it by mail or the Internet through a series of lessons and quizzes that are returned with grades and comments for each student. This course then prepares them for certification through our national organization.

Wright

Here's the major question: How do you assess personality and skills through handwriting?

Sassi

Handwriting is just another form of self-expression. How we write is just one more projection of who we are. For example, someone with very large handwriting would indicate a person who likes a lot of activity, is ego driven, and would probably be a dynamic leader, while small, concise handwriting would indicate a person who is more detail-oriented and good with facts and figures, probably a good organizational manager.

Donald Trump's writing shows dynamics and ego drive.

Albert Einstein's writing displays concentration, analytical ability and attention to detail.

Wright

I've noticed that I have two distinct signatures when I sign things, one when I'm in a hurry and one when I'm not.

Sassi

Your signature is your public persona. So when you're in a hurry, it's probably more elaborated and scribbled, with perhaps a long line after it. We call it executive caution; you're holding people at arm's distance. In other words, you are saying, "Go away; leave me alone; I'm in a hurry." And the other signature is probably more legible, and you're saying, "This is who I am; let's sit and talk."

Wright

You're right. When I start writing, I put a great big "D" then the "a-v-i-d" is hardly legible; then a big "W" and the "r-i-g-h-t" is hardly legible. And you're right . . . there's a line after it.

Sassi

Yes, and the big capitals would also indicate your confidence and leadership skills.

Wright

And the accuracy of that would be?

Sassi

How do we establish the accuracy?

Wright

Yes.

Sassi

It has been handed down through the ages. Abbe Michon, a French priest, who correlated people's behavior with strokes in their writing, first established the term "graphology." Other graphologists have put strokes together into traits, and it has evolved from there.

Wright

Paula, I was fascinated by your lecture topic "Personnel Analysis." What are some of the indicators you look for when your clients need to find qualified management, administrative, and sales personnel?

Sassi

Assessing personality in handwriting is really based on three building blocks. Arrangement, which is how the writing is placed on the paper, indicates a writer's organizational skills and clarity of thought. Form is the actual letter connections and formations and also the form level, meaning how rhythmical and symmetrical the writing looks. Movement, then, is the speed and pressure of the writing, which indicates how fast the writer processes information and how intense and energetic they are in their efforts. On a finer scale, we go into the strokes by simply correlating the strokes with personality traits.

Wright

So when you say placement, you mean when they are writing on the line, above the line, or below it?

Sassi

Exactly, and usually when I request a writing sample for an analysis, I ask for it on unlined paper, because we want to see where that baseline is going. The line of writing tells us a lot about the writer's emotional mood and control. If the line is moving upward, the writer is positive and optimistic; if the line is moving downward, the writer may be negative or pessimistic. Then we also look at the margins: Are they reaching out to the future, or are they pulling back? The right margin is the future; the left margin is the past. So sometimes I find writers who have all the attributes for the job, but their right margin is wide and I conclude that they are great for the position, but they really don't want the job because they are apprehensive about it. This has proven itself more times than my clients like to admit. The writing doesn't have to be neat; you know, people immediately say, "Oh, my writing is such a mess." Well, that shows an expressive type, ready to get moving, get out there. So the form level isn't always exactly what they think is neatness, like the copybook we learned in school. Copybook is just our base measure, and then, as the writing deviates from copybook and changes, it shows how the writer has matured since childhood.

Wright

So if I wrote you a letter on unlined paper, you could determine the lines that I'm making?

Sassi

I could determine your emotional state at the time that you wrote it. And there, too, we want to take into consideration if this a state or a trait. Is the writer just in a state of feeling bad, or feeling highly energetic that day, or is it a trait that is always in his or her personality? I, therefore, put a disclaimer in my reports that states that the findings are based on the mood of the writer at the time the writing sample was written.

Wright

So it's like testing; it would be better to have more samples?

Sassi

Yes, but that's not always possible. I use a form called a "Skills Summary Supplement" that asks the applicant to give handwritten answers to four relevant questions about the job. This gives me enough writing to analyze.

Wright

Your programs are very interesting, especially the ones that talk about the ability to discover "red flags" of deception and dishonesty. Could you tell us a little about that?

Sassi

One of the major traits my clients want me to identify is the honesty and reliability of a writer, whether it's an analysis pertaining to their personal life or for business. There are a number of dishonesty factors that can be found in the handwriting, and they really jump out at me when I see them in a sample. They deal with different areas of the personality, whether it's how the person thinks, acts, or feels. For example, left hooks at the beginning stroke of a letter often indicate the possibility of theft. And that's very important to many of my clients.

Left beginning hooks indicate acquisitiveness.

Highly embellished "A's" and "O's" that contain hooks or loops or angles can indicate some type of verbal dishonesty or manipulation.

Elaborated lower loops—for example, the "Y's" or "G's"—can be signs of subconscious guilt, insatiable needs, or greediness. Lower loops represent the subconscious area of the personality that is not always discernable just by meeting and talking to someone.

Wright

If someone studied this and knew the things that you just said, could they mask their handwriting?

Sassi

Not really. What happens then is they try to make it too perfect, and a very major indicator of dishonesty is very slow writing. This dishonesty factor would come out, and I have had that happen.

Wright

So being slow and deliberate would be almost a cover-up?

Sassi

Correct.

Wright

What types of clients do you have? In other words, do businesses and individuals seek you out to help them?

Sassi

They really do, and I have every kind of business that you can think of. Most of my clients seek me out either through the phone book or the Internet, or they hear me give a presentation, or are referred to me. They range from small business owners to Fortune 500 companies. Usually hiring a sales force is their number one interest, whether it is insurance, car sales, or promotional businesses such as permanent and temporary placement agencies. Then, of course, people in general use me too. They may be checking out their new boyfriend or girlfriend. I get a lot of requests from future father-in-laws and mother-in-laws, because they're not too sure about the person their son or daughter is hooking up with.

Wright

You're kidding.

Sassi

No, they take it very seriously too.

Wright

I don't want to put you on the spot but, I remember reading about—and perhaps we talked about—you giving characteristics of some handwriting samples of famous people. Could you give us an idea of what you're talking about?

Sassi

Well, recently, with the current news, I did a full report on the anthrax letters, and I have also been on TV analyzing the signature of Osama Bin Laden. Just recently I received the handwriting of Kenneth Lay in the Enron scandal. And I've also done, when it was big news, the O.J. Simpson suicide letter. I was on TV analyzing that as well.

The symbolic signature of Osama Bin Laden looks like the outline of a machine gun with many other symbols within its form.

Wright

And there were distinguishing characteristics of the handwriting?

Sassi

Amazingly so; and if anybody is interested in either of these cases, they can contact me. The article on the anthrax letters was published in an investigators' newsletter.

Wright

Do you have a website that they could go to, or telephone number?

Sassi

Yes . . . www.handwritingconsultants.com, or they can contact me at 858-586-1511.

Wright

So it's www.handwritingconsultants.com.

Sassi

Right, and soon I will have the articles on that website. I also did an article on jury screening, because I do jury selection as well.

Wright

In some of the larger areas, some of the bigger trials, jury selection committees have gotten to be a big, big business.

Sassi

Oh, yes, they do things like measure eye blinks and things like that.

Wright

Exactly.

Sassi

But I can do it on the handwriting, even if they only have a signature and a check mark. Everyone will make that check mark differently. How big it is, how angled it is, all tells me something.

Wright

With our *Mission Possible!* talk show and book, we are trying to encourage people in our audience to be better, live better, and be more fulfilled by listening to the examples of our guests. Is there anyone or anything in your life that has made a difference for you and helped you to be a better person?

Sassi

Well, really, my clients have been my inspiration. Most of them are highly successful business owners who value my input and look beyond the traditional ways of managing their enterprise, which really makes me feel confident in myself. They encourage me to continue in my work, because it serves them well and it provides the information they need to stay on top. Though we start out at a business consulting level, I sometimes help them with their personal or family problems, so even people who are highly successful have their down moments. We just discuss it on the phone, and they fax me over the handwriting of perhaps their problem child or family members who are going through some bad times, and I help get them through it.

Wright

So I would imagine that confidentiality would be very, very important in your business.

Sassi

Oh, yes, that's right. If it is highly confidential, I don't even mention the name in the report. I just refer to "the writing you submitted for analysis."

Wright

So when you're interpreting personality traits, it would be important to, number one, know what you are doing, and number two, be very, very confidential about it.

Sassi

Yes, that's right.

Wright

What do you think makes up a great mentor? These clients that you're talking about, especially the ones that help you or encourage you, in other words, are there characteristics that mentors seem to have in common?

Sassi

Well, you know, I think any one can be a mentor if they can learn to look beyond themselves. The best mentors for me have been people who see a little of themselves in me or see themselves in others and they want to help people to achieve the same level of success that they have. The best mentors that I've had mainly are the ones that stick with me through the good and bad times and help brainstorm to find solutions to what seems to be monumental problems.

Wright

Do people that you are associated with in your business swap handwriting samples to ascertain whether or not as a group that you're doing the same thing?

Sassi

Sometimes, yes, but what I do is I have an assistant who helps me, and I bounce it off her; and when there are some that are really interesting, I fax them over to another friend—yes, we do that quite often. We also share the famous handwritings that come up in the news. So we always find a resource for that. We have an international handwriting analysis review that comes out with very informative articles in it. We also have a convention every year; this year it's going to be in Canada, and I'm going to be installed as the president of the organization that certified me.

Wright

Oh, my! Congratulations!

Sassi

Thank you.

Wright

I can close my eyes and see Abraham Lincoln's signature. I can also close my eyes and see Richard Nixon's signature, and I wonder about them, because the signatures are so different.

Sassi

Well, they were men of different times too. Abraham Lincoln's signature is very controlled, intellectual-looking, Spencerian type writing, but I have seen Abraham Lincoln's writing samples on a good day and on a bad day.

It is interesting that you bring up Nixon, because I use his writing in my talks. I use his signature and how his signatures changed while going through the Watergate Scandal and when he had to leave office, but then how the signature came back to it's usual level of pride afterwards. Presidents sometimes have very threaded writing, which indicates their diplomacy and evasiveness.

Abraham Lincoln's writing shows his intellectual and calm style.

That must be yours to have laid so costly a sacrif
upon the altar of freedom
  Yours very sincerely and respectfully
    A. Lincoln

Wright

Nixon, after all his troubles, finally at the end of his life, was an elder statesman.

Sassi

Yes, and it showed in his signature as well. It's very interesting how it deteriorated and then evolved back.

Wright

That is interesting.

Sassi

And it's all because at the end of all his writing, he has a right hook, not a left hook, which shows tenacity, and that's what got him through.

Wright

Most people thought that he would either kill himself or die very quickly after he left office, but they were wrong.

Sassi

That's right.

Richard Nixon's signatures during Watergate and beyond.

A 1969 presidential signature.

Later, a change had begun.

1974—A final signature before leaving the White House.

1989—on the comeback trail.

Wright

Most people are fascinated with the new TV shows about being a survivor. What has been the greatest comeback you have made from adversity in your career or life?

Sassi

Well, I'm afraid it happened to me just a few years ago. My business took a very serious dip because of corporate "buy outs." The new owners didn't want to continue with my services, but I survived by finding an alternative source of income while building my business back up to a more productive level. And even the people who sold their corporations still stuck by me and helped me to find new clients. And when things seem to go slow, I just tell myself, "Okay, the day is not over." It's just amazing how something comes my way, maybe in the form of a late-night call or an unexpected contact. So you know, when I'm having one of those bad days or think that business is slow, I just say, "The day is not over. Something's coming."

Wright

Do your clients basically network with you or for you?

Sassi

Oh, yes! It's been wonderful. They recommend me to someone else, and I join networking groups as well to get the word out, because people are skeptical of handwriting analysis. However, when I can actually sit people down and show them the basics of handwriting analysis, they say "Of course, this just makes sense." And so that helps me to get more clients and educate people to the high level that I am capable of working at with this. You know, you can have a lot of hobbyists in this field, too, which is fine, but it really takes years to become proficient and comfortable with it, and I'm still constantly learning.

Wright

I remember the first time I talked to you I couldn't help but think how, many years ago, people would talk about chiropractors, and it sounded like voodoo. And now, millions of people who are helped by chiropractors can't be wrong, can they?

Sassi

I love chiropractors; I had breakfast with my chiropractor this morning.

Wright

I can remember when they were regarded much lower than medical doctors, and now people are beginning to treat them with respect.

Sassi

Anything new generates a certain amount of skepticism and resentment, because people don't want you coming into their territory. Handwriting analysis is so much easier than dealing with reams of testing and lengthy interviews. It just saves a lot of the management time. If we can narrow it down with the handwriting in hiring, we can focus on the ones that are really qualified for the job.

Wright

One of the major topics in our country today—it has been for several decades and will probably be for decades to come—is the educational system. I understand you facilitate workshops for teachers and educators.

Sassi

Yes, I do. I just did one recently in Texas. Children's handwriting and drawings can be analyzed for learning disabilities, behavioral problems, and personality or family issues. We actually help children by first working on their gross motor skills, so it doesn't have to do with their writing at first. Then we lead up to facilitating the fine motor skills necessary for writing and general dexterity. I work in conjunction with a developmental motor skill specialist; she's a teacher and she tutors children. She and I have developed a video which we entitled "Exercises for Education." On it, my daughter is actually doing the demonstration and the teacher is telling her what to do as she demonstrates exercises for body balance. Then large writing movements are done in the air and on a board, and we graduate them to what we call our mirror books. They're still not writing; they are just mirroring the forms and images to achieve right and left brain balance. The next step is to finally use my books, which are called the *Write Approach* books, 1 and 2, that teach handwriting movement. So you see, with this method we are teaching children how to get in balance with their bodies. Once they have achieved body/brain balance, you can sit them down and teach them handwriting.

Wright

How do you help teachers better understand their student's emotional blocks to learning?

Sassi

We have a test called the Hepner Writing Test. It is administered by simply having the child write a row of angles, which looks like little pyramids; a row of garland, which looks like little cups; and a row of upside down cups, which we call arcades.

How the child makes these forms tells us about their basic attitudes. The angles tell us their attitude toward work; the cups tell us their emotional level; for example, if the cups are very flat, then maybe they're not feeling loved enough. And the really revealing one is the upside down cups, the arcades. When they cannot make these arcades well, that means they have trouble going within themselves to calm themselves and learn. It's just amazing, because I've used it on children as old as fourteen years old, and they still make very ill-formed arcades. These children generally have some type of hyperactivity problem.

The Hepner Writing Test

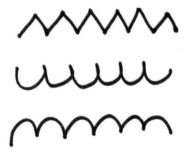

Wright

At some point and time, is this information shared with the parents?

Sassi

Of course, this information is given to the parents in the initial assessment results.

Wright

I could almost imagine that in the event that you got the child early enough, you might modify a bad behavior into good behavior?

Sassi

Yes, and hopefully, in time, we'll be able to eliminate terms like attention deficient disorder or dyslexia. So we recommend these therapies be used with children between the ages of six and twelve.

Wright

I have talked to two very famous people in the past few months who were diagnosed with dyslexia, both of them at age thirty-seven. In both cases their teachers had taught them that they were dumb, so that's what they thought. Simply through chance someone diagnosed them, and their life changed from then on.

Sassi

It's not so much the learning disability, but it's the emotional damage they suffer because of it. And it causes them to act out, or have no self-esteem, and it's really sad.

Wright

If you could have a platform and tell our audience something you feel that would help or encourage them, what would you say?

Sassi

I would borrow a phrase from Joseph Campbell, which is, "Follow your bliss." Pursue what you enjoy doing, and then turn it into a career or business.

You know I never thought I would be making a living at handwriting analysis, because I was just looking for a hobby. But this interesting hobby turned into a vehicle for me to make presentations all over the world, write books ,and consult with some of the most amazing business people in the country and in the world. So it's been a great ride.

Wright

When you talk to a CEO of a very successful business, you're probably talking to someone who could probably teach you a lot.

Sassi

Oh, they do; as I said, they are my mentors.

Wright

Well, we have come down to end of our program, and I really do appreciate the conversation today.

Sassi

Thank you, I consider you as one of my mentors too.

Wright

Well good! What is the study of handwriting called?

Sassi

Graphology.

Wright

Graphology. The entire study of graphology is really fascinating, and I can just imagine some of our listeners—and I know some of our readers—will probably take some adult courses like you did.

Sassi

Well, just tell them to get in touch with me, and we'll get them signed up.

Wright

We have been talking today to Paula Sassi, who has been a professional in the field of handwriting analysis since 1980. She is the owner and director of her own company and serves some fascinating clients, and we have found out today why she is a fascinating lady.

Paula, thank you so much for being on *Mission Possible!*

Sassi

Thank you.

Paula A. Sassi, C.G.
9715 Caminito Doha
San Diego, CA 92131
(858) 586-1511 or (800) 880-1511
Fax: (858) 695-8526
E-mail: hci@hotmail.com
www.handwritingconsultants.com

Chapter 9

Brian Moran

Brian Moran is founder and president of Strategic Breakthroughs. A visionary and strategic thinker, Brian has over twenty years of expertise as a corporate executive, entrepreneur, coach and speaker. His experience includes positions as president and CEO of a start-up venture as well as corporate vice president of sales and service for a billion dollar company. Brian is the driving force behind many of the successful executives and entrepreneurs in industry today. He is the leading expert on execution and has developed a proven performance system that ensures effective implementation and greater results.

The Interview

David Wright (Wright)

Today we are talking to Brian Moran, founder and president of Strategic Breakthroughs. With over twenty years' experience as a corporate executive, entrepreneur, consultant, and coach, Brian's breakthrough approach to success has been tried and proven in his own business, giving him the impetus to share his principles and methods with individuals and organizations who desire greater achievements and growth. Brian received a Bachelor of Science in business administration from the University of Phoenix. As a speaker, Brian is thought provoking and passionate as he teaches action-based concepts and strategies. Brian, welcome to *Mission Possible!*

Brian Moran (Moran)

Thanks. Glad to be with you.

Wright

Brian, tell us a little bit about your company, Strategic Breakthroughs. That's a great name. What do you do, specifically?

Moran

I work with managers, entrepreneurs, and sales professionals on improving performance. Now that is a fairly broad topic, the specific way in which I bring value is by focusing on execution. My experience over the years has been that most individuals, most organizations don't hurt for good ideas. But where the rubber meets the road is how well they implement. And I've developed a system that helps organizations and individuals execute more effectively, a system that helps them implement their best ideas.

Wright

Do you run into people in corporations who are just brilliant and have all kinds of ideas all the time, but never know how to put wheels on them and make them roll or wings to make them fly?

Moran

That's exactly right. And you know, the reality is that the market leaders don't necessarily have better ideas; they just implement more effectively. The brutal reality is the marketplace couldn't care less about your ideas. The only thing the marketplace rewards is what gets implemented. So that's the focus.

Wright

I was interested in a question that you posed in one of your programs titled "The Game of Work." The question was, What would the average American say is more motivating and fun, work or sports? I can imagine what kind of response you get, but what kind of point are you trying to make?

Moran

It's an interesting question, because when I pose that to people, it causes them to stop and think about that for a moment. I ask them, "Can you imagine people—fans—paying for the privilege of seeing you in action?" You can imagine the response. The analogy here is that one of the things that makes sports so motivating is the fact that we keep score. I've been watching the Olympics, and the games are fascinating; but if you took away the scoring, whether that may be the time or whatever kind of scoring system there is, it would not be nearly as motivating. A football game without the end zones, without the goal posts, without the score board, and just a football out there with twenty-two guys, what kind of crowd is that going to attract? We recognize that in sports; let's apply that same methodology to business.

So often people end their day without knowing if they won or lost. They don't even know if they scored, whereas if you look at sports, scoring is dynamic. Furthermore, no one needs to tell the players when they score. The player that crosses the goal line doesn't need to go up and ask the coach, "Hey, did I score?" You see, the fans know instantly, the players know instantly, the coach knows instantly. So how do we create that same kind of dynamic scoring in business?

Wright

Right. I've been glued to the Olympics. I was watching the men's downhill last night, and the gold medalist beat the second place finisher by .02 of a second. Unbelievable!

Moran

Yes, incredible.

Wright

You stated in one of your writings that students in the public school system who are graded through direct instructions scored higher academically and on self-esteem than those who are not tested at all. Is there a movement in society to do away with testing?

Moran

There seems to be, to some degree. The notion is that we want everyone to feel good and have high self-esteem, and I think the intent is good. We want to build children's self-esteem. The reality is that measurement and scoring actually contribute to the development of self-esteem.

Moran

Back in the fifties and sixties, when industrial psychologists began to study motivation, Fredrick Herzberg was a professor at Utah and did over two thousand studies and observations to determine what motivates people in the work place, and he narrowed it down to the top two motivators: achievement and recognition. Now, I submit that the only way you know if you're achieving is if you're measuring, so the article that you mentioned was an interesting article in that the researchers compared kids that were schooled in direct instruction—that being right answer/wrong answer and tests—with kids that were not receiving tests and grades as part of their educational experience. They found that those kids who were schooled in direct instruction indeed scored higher academically, which was somewhat expected. What surprised them is that the kids who were schooled in direct instruction, the kids that were being scored, also had higher self-esteem. The notion that keeping score somehow damages self-esteem is just not the case; in fact, it happens to be just the opposite. Keeping score actually builds self-esteem.

Wright

That is amazing. The school that my thirteen-year-old daughter attends tries to make everyone feel comfortable. I'm trying to get my daughter to focus and make better grades.

Moran

You know, it's funny, because the soccer league for the really young kids around my neighborhood doesn't keep score. But you know what? At the end of the game, every kid knows the score.

Wright

You bet.

Moran

And they don't walk away all that dejected. I was unfortunate enough as a youngster to play on a Little League baseball team that was awful. We were absolutely terrible. But we started tracking if we got more hits or runs or made fewer errors, things like that. That became the motivator for us.

Wright

My son was a great football player when he was just a little fellow playing in Little League. He played on a championship team that had a quarterback who played both offense and defense, so my son sat on the bench most of the time. All the other coaches would come over and want him to play for them as their starting quarterback, but he refused, saying, "I want to be a champion."

Moran

Oh, great attitude!

Wright

In your presentation "Execution Is the Key," you quote Michael Dell, of Dell Computers, who was asked if he was concerned about his business model being copied. Do you remember his response? And can you give us the layman's view of your performance system?

Moran

Sure. Michael actually responded with, "Not at all. I know we will execute it better!" which is an interesting response. Michael Dell understands what may be the most important concept in business, and that is, it's not what you know, it's not who you know; it's what you implement. And the performance system is designed to help organizations and individuals do just that—to execute more effectively. We apply it at the organizational level with the leadership team, but also at the individual level, especially with sales professionals/producers. And it's really the same mode.

There are four primary components to it, David. The first is what I call effective mental models, and that's the notion that we create things twice: first mentally, then physically. The biggest barrier of high performance is not the physical manifestation but the mental creation, because when we really stretch our vision of what's possible, we bump up against what I call the gremlins. You know that conversation, that mental conversation that says some version of "No way, not possible." And the reality is that we only create things physically that we first create mentally. Roger Bannister is an example I like to use here. I don't know if you recall that name.

Wright

Yes, he was the first man to break the four-minute mile.

Moran

There you go; yes. And what was interesting about that is up until that time everyone said it was impossible. In fact, the medical community came out and said that man as a species is not built to do that.

Wright

Right.

Moran

What's most fascinating, though, is that after he broke through the record, in the next couple of years hundreds of other people did as well. And we're seeing that today with the Olympics. Even in physical events, the barrier is not physical; it's mental. It's the same in business. So the first component of the system is to create effective mental models, to stretch our vision of what's possible to the point where we bump up against some of those limiting beliefs and then be able to look at those as not right or wrong, not good or bad—just identify them for what they are. There's a continuum that I like to use, and that's the notion that our results are produced by our actions, and our actions are driven by our thinking or beliefs. It's our thinking or beliefs that ultimately drive our results.

And the interesting thing is, so often we focus on the actions—you know, if I want a different result, I take a different action, and that's absolutely true. However, if the new action is incongruent with an existing belief, then we're not going to be very successful with that action. We won't stay in a state of incongruence, so oftentimes we'll revert back to the old action. We tend to beat ourselves up and say, "Boy, I'm just not disciplined." Well, the reality is, our belief system—our thinking—doesn't support the new action. In addition, our thinking is a little like water to a fish in that it tends to be transparent. Rarely do we think about our thinking. But if the thinking shifts, everything shifts. If our beliefs shift, everything shifts. That's the notion of effective mental models; that's where breakthrough occurs, at the belief level, not the action level.

Wright

Right.

Moran

The second component, then, is planning. As we stretch that vision of what's possible, and we begin to challenge ourselves around what greatness looks like, then we need to build a plan to achieve it. What I found to be most effective is that we plan at a number of levels: three years, one year, ninety days, weekly. It's a building block approach that seems to provide a solid road map with long enough time frames that we can get things done, but short enough that there's some impetus to get rolling on it.

The third component is really around implementation, and there I found that we tend to rely on discipline, so what we've done here is create a process and tools that we can rely on. We also tap into what Herzberg found about what is motivating, so that weekly plan that I mentioned in the planning phase also becomes a weekly scorecard—we're scoring our execution. I score whether I did what I said was most important to the long-term profitability and viability of my business.

Wright

Right.

Moran

The fourth component is what I call key measures. That's the reality check. That's where we look and say, "Okay, what's the physical universe telling us about what we are doing?" Whereas at the implementation component we measure "Did we do it?" here we measure "Is it producing?"

Wright

I used to tell the people in my company, "If you can't set annual goals, set goals for six months; if not six months, then three; if not three, then one." Finally we would get down to hourly goals.

Moran

Yes.

Wright

The most important thing is to learn how to set goals.

Moran

Yes, and those metrics on how we measure it, those monthly and weekly indicators, are critical.

Wright

I see.

Moran

Because what we don't want to do is find out after it's too late. Let me go back to sports now. Can you imagine playing a football game and not keeping score throughout the game, just finding out at the end when they announce it that you lost by three points? Again, the notion of dynamic scoring. So how did we do this week? How did we do this month?

Wright

Yes.

Moran

What I found is that a lot of people go off to conferences and come back with great ideas. They tend not to fully implement the ideas, and then three or four months later they say, "You know, this stuff doesn't work. I need new ideas."

Wright

Right.

Moran

Whereas with this system, we know that if we identify an exciting idea, it's going to get implemented, and we're going to measure it. If it's producing, great; we continue to implement it. If it's not, then we've got to go back and look at the content of the plan.

Wright

You talk a lot about creativity. Are there certain people born with it, or can anyone develop creativity?

Moran

Yes and yes. I mean, I think we're all born with it. There certainly are some folks that have a greater capacity for it, where they may be almost gifted in the area of creativity, and we probably all know some of those. I think the other thing I've experienced with the majority of folks, though, is that the average person is much more creative than they might think they are. Creativity is one of those capabilities that the more you exercise it, the stronger it becomes. So I believe we're all born with that capability; how often we use it and how we challenge it within ourselves makes a big difference, but I believe it's available to everyone, and probably the average person is much more creative in everyday life than he or she realizes.

Wright

In reading a lot about you and your work, in preparation for this interview, I came upon the "5 Steps to Creativity" that you teach. Could you give us a quick overview of the steps?

Moran

Sure, I'd love to. The five I think make a big difference in terms of cultivating creativity are as follows: One, suspend judgment. There's a tendency to just judge things out of the box and assume that you know it won't work. With the people that are most creative, it's an entirely different mindset; it's a much more curious mindset. You need to learn to suspend that judgment. We are really back to those mental models I spoke of earlier; our thinking creates our experience in life. So the biggest barrier to creativity is just our thinking and the tendency some have to look for what is wrong with a new idea, as opposed to looking for what's right. Instead, take a curious stand: What if? What if we could do that? What would be different? Don't worry initially about why it won't work, but look for the things that might work. So number one would be to suspend judgment.

The second point is be willing to fail. Most judgment comes from a fear of failing. We don't want to fail, so we decide not to risk; we play it safe, and the safer we play, the less creative we are. The other thing that happens is, the less risk we take, the more sensitive we become to failure.

Wright

I see.

Moran

You know, failure is not bad. It does not define you.

Wright

I hope not.

Moran

Thomas Edison failed over nine thousand times in his experiments to invent electric light. At what point was he a failure? Was it his thousandth try? Was it his eight thousand and twenty-ninth try?

Wright

Great question.

Moran

The point being, failure is not bad. So in order to cultivate creativity, 1) suspend judgment; 2), be willing to fail; and 3), learn to create multiple solutions. When we're faced with a scenario, there's a tendency to identify a solution and then run with it. I would suggest that you always identify at least two solutions. Oftentimes that second solution is much more effective than the first one. So number three would be, create multiple solutions.

Number four is pay attention. Observation is powerful! Being in the moment without distraction is amazing; it's incredible what you notice that you might otherwise overlook. New elements emerge, new possibilities. Attention leads to curiosity; curiosity leads to creativity.

Wright

Right.

Moran

So we have suspend judgment, be willing to fail, create multiple solutions, and pay attention. The fifth and last step for cultivating creativity is think "both-and." If we want to tap into our creativity, we need to stop thinking "either-or" and start thinking "both-and." So often we get stuck thinking things either have to be A or B. We can have it this way or that way. We either can have change or stability. We can either make more money or have more family time. Stop thinking either-or and start thinking both-and.

Wright

I remember reading in one of your exercises that if you draw a horizontal line through an eight, you come up with zero, and if you draw a vertical line through an eight, you come up with a three.

Moran

Yes.

Wright

So you can have it both ways and have more than one answer.

Moran

Yes, that's a great example. When I ask people, "What's half of eight?" they go for the numeric answer: four.

Wright

Right.

Moran

And I say, "Yes, that's one right answer. What's another right answer?" So there again, you're challenged to be creative. You know if you divide it different ways, you come up with different answers. And depending on the scenario, three might be a better answer than four.

Wright

Years ago, I was reading something about Edison. Some Eastern writer asked him how it felt to fail two or three thousand times. He said, "I didn't fail. I found two thousand ways that did not work."

Moran

Absolutely.

Wright

Didn't deter him, obviously.

Moran

Yes, that's a great example of commitment. You know, when the question of "if" goes away, it's just a question of "how."

Wright

Brian, with our Mission Possible! talk show and book, we're trying to encourage people in our audience to be better, to live better, and to be more fulfilled by listening to the examples of our guests. Is there anything or anyone in your life who has made a difference for you and helped you to become a better person?

Moran

Absolutely, quite a few folks, in fact, and I would suspect , that's true for most people. The first person that comes to my mind is my dad. My dad had a huge impact in my life. I lost my dad to cancer about five years ago; it was a terrible struggle and probably the most difficult thing I've ever been through. But I still remember my dad, ever since we were little, encouraging us to always give a hundred percent. "If you're going to do it," he would say, "give it one hundred percent or don't do it at all." Make the choice to do it, and once you make that choice, then give it your all. And that has served me well in just about everything I do.

Wright

I have done a lot of leadership conferences the last several years, and I always ask people to write down the five people that have impacted their life the most, and it's odd—about three of the top five are teachers. I hope that's going to be the same in another decade or two. But I know for me, teachers were really great role models and helped me out a lot. Your dad sounds like quite a guy.

Moran

Yes, he was. The second individual on my list is a teacher also. It's funny you mentioned that. Yes, a teacher and my football coach, same guy.

Wright

Same guy?

Moran

Yes.

Wright

Is he still living?

Moran

He's not. No.

Wright

Up until he died, what did you call him?

Moran

Coach.

Wright

That's interesting. That is a term of endearment.

Moran

Oh, yes.

Wright

I was talking yesterday to Stephen Covey—we're about the same age I think. We were kind of reminiscing, and I told him, "You know, 'Coach' is really a term of respect. I called my seventh grade coach 'Coach' until I was in my fifties." After he died, I would never think of calling him by his name, not even "Mister." To me, "Mister" is not as respectful as "Coach."

Moran

That's right. It's a term of endearment, that's for certain.

Wright

What do you think makes up a great mentor? In other words, are there characteristics that mentors seem to have in common?

Moran

Yes, I think so. As I think about it—I'll probably miss some of them—but one that comes to mind is that I think great mentors are caring. As I think about the mentors in my life, they've been caring. Caring about the whole person—not just about a particular aspect, but genuinely, "How are you doing? What are you struggling with?" Another common characteristic I think great mentors have is that they are honest and candid—almost to the degree of being brutal at times. You know, helping you see areas where you have blind spots, things that you're just not facing. Acknowledging the reality of the situation. I think great mentors are encouraging.

Wright

Right.

Moran

You know, there are times when we all hit the wall, times when we're all struggling, and mentors seem to have a sense of when that is and the ability to come up alongside of you and just say that thing or just do that thing that kind of carries you through the day. The other aspect, David, that comes to mind when I think about mentoring is that great mentors tend to have a skill or ability to help you discover things. The great mentors that I've experienced are not preaching to you; they're typically asking some really deep questions that are helping you discover the answers for yourself. And probably the overriding thing, I think, about mentors is their willingness to invest in you. You know, life-on-life investments.

Wright

Years ago, I read a book on mentors by a woman whose name I've forgotten. She was talking about mentors and saying basically what you are saying—you called it brutal; she said it was like being an oyster, irritated all the time; but in the final analysis, through that irritation, she came out a shiny pearl.

Moran

Yes. That's a great metaphor.

Wright

And so you're right; sometimes brutal mentors can be *really* brutal.

Moran

Yes, I think so.

Wright

You know, most people are fascinated with these new TV shows about being a survivor. What has been the greatest comeback you have made from adversity in your career or in your life?

Moran

Careerwise it would be the time I got involved with a start-up company. I had a position as corporate VP in sales and service with a billion dollar retailer and left there and got involved in a start-up company where I was president and CEO and one of the four primary investors. And we struggled considerably with that company. It was a scenario where I got involved and I didn't understand the fundamentals of the business. I came there with the general management experience and set up the marketing system and everything, but I didn't know enough about the business to know exactly where our services should be focused. In addition, it ended up being a much more capital intensive business than we thought. So I went from corporate America, with a nice, big paycheck and stocks, to not being able to cash checks and really struggling through that scenario and beginning to question my abilities. It was really the first time in my career that I had ever struggled to that degree. And it really caused me to take stock and say, "Wait a minute. Does this struggle define me as a person? Is it who I am?" Happy to say, that business is existing today. It's profitable. I'm still a shareholder and involved strategically, just not day to day. But it took a lot to get through that. It tested me in so many ways. I think probably the greatest thing it did for me is that it built my character. You know, it's easy to be positive when things are going well.

Wright

Right.

Moran

How do you maintain that outlook when things are rough?

Wright

If you could have a platform and tell our audience something that you feel would help or encourage them, what would you say?

Moran

How much time do I have?

Wright

Oh, about a minute and thirty seconds.

Moran

Oh, okay, a couple of things. As I watched the Olympics, I've pondered the question of greatness. The work I do with people is really about helping them maximize their potential, about helping them get to what "great" looks like for them. So I asked myself, When does one become great? Is it when you achieve the end result? Is it when you win the gold medal, or when you achieve a certain result in business, or an income level?

I would submit that that is not when you become great. That is simply the evidence of your greatness. Rather, greatness happens in a moment, in an instant, when we choose to do the things we need to do. The difference between mediocre and great on a daily, weekly basis is very slim. The difference in results in six months, one year, three years out is fantastic, but on a daily, weekly basis it's pretty slim.

What's powerful about that for me is the understanding that I can be great starting today, and as long as I continue to do those things—the things I need to do—that will be reflected in my results somewhere down the line, but I'm great this moment. It's not something I have to wait for.

So, to the listeners out there, you can be great starting now; it's not going to take you a year or two. The results may not show till then, but the greatness happens in a moment.

Wright

Well, we have come down to the end of a half hour. Can you believe that?

Moran

No, that was quick.

Wright

Today, we have been talking to Brian Moran, founder and president of Strategic Breakthroughs. He is a speaker, trainer, consultant, and coach, and as you have learned today, a very bright individual with some great, great information for all of us. So Brian, thank you so much for being a part of *Mission Possible!* today.

Moran

Thanks for having me. I've enjoyed it.

Brian Moran
Strategic Breakthroughs
913 W. Holmes, Suite 220E
Lansing, MI 48910
(517) 393-0765
E-mail: Brian@strategicbreakthroughs.net
www.strategicbreakthroughs.net

Chapter 10

Bill Blades

Bill Blades, CMC, CPS, is a professional speaker and consultant specializing in the areas of leadership, creativity and sales management. He is the author of Top Gun Selling: Winning Tactics of the Top 2% of Salespeople.

The Interview

David E. Wright (Wright)

Today we are talking to Bill Blades, a professional speaker, trainer, consultant, and author. Bill speaks from experience. While serving as vice president of sales and marketing for a food manufacturing company, he increased sales 150%, from thirteen million to thirty-three million, in only four years. His firm was named Small Business of the Year. He also served as Finance Chairman for Newt Gingrich, former Speaker of the House of the United States Congress. Bill is the author of the best-selling book

Selling: The Mother of All Enterprise, as well as featured with attorney F. Lee Bailey in the book *Leadership Strategists.* He has served on the faculties of The Graduate School of Banking of the South, College of Estate Planning Attorneys, National Association of Sales Professionals, and lectures at universities, including the number one-rated international graduate school in the U.S., American Graduate School of International Management. He is also a member of the National Speakers Association.

Bill Blades, welcome to *Mission Possible!*

Bill Blades (Blades)

David, thank you very much.

Wright

Bill, I was interested in your presentation *Selling—It's a Whole-Brainer.* Does that have to do with the right-brain/left-brain theory?

Blades

It does, right side being the creative side and left side being the logical side. The one thing I'd like our listeners to appreciate is that more sales come from right-brain selling and thinking than from left-side selling and thinking. I think most of our listeners would agree that most business phone calls are boring. Most business letters are boring, and there's a tremendous amount of salespeople that come off as boring. So there's one answer to the puzzle: Don't be boring. Most salespeople walk in and visit a client and on the first visit will say things like, "Hi, how are you?" The standard answer that comes back is "Fine." You really don't want a meeting to start out with "fine."

This is the way I have always done it. I like to call the assistant a couple of days before my appointment and say, "Can I ask for your help? I have an appointment with Mr. Big on Thursday. Can you tell me what he likes in a salesperson? Can you tell me what he doesn't like in a salesperson?" I then send over a gift of appreciation to the assistant. The assistant has got that sales call set up for me by telling Mr. Big, "You're going to like that Bill Blades."

When calling to get the appointment, it goes like this: "Sure, Bill, you can come in Thursday anytime between 8 A.M. and 12." I say, "Great; let me have the 8:03." Well, already their eyeballs are twitching a little bit. So then I confirm the appointment with a postcard that's got four bullets on it. It says, "I'll be there Thursday the 29th at 7:59 for my 8:03." So usually when I show up, that person and sometimes other people are standing in the lobby with the postcard. There are two things they want to see: one, what time I show up, and number two, they want to see who this screwball is.

So the message that I sent to them is I'm going to come in with a lot of right-brain thinking, and I'm not going to come in like a duck, like everybody else that makes an appointment at 8:00, 9:00 or 10:00, and then they show up and say, "Hi, how are you?" That's right-brain selling.

Wright

You're saying that the right brain is the creative side, and to be noticed and appreciated you've always got to be creative?

Blades

Exactly.

Wright

In your presentation, you say that being different makes a difference in sales and marketing. What do you mean by that?

Blades

First, we have to set ourselves apart from the crowd. Unfortunately, many people refuse to use creativity because logically they're talking themselves out of doing new things. Their left brain is interfering with the right brain. It's almost like the stars are out there during the daytime, but the sun interferes. What happens is, people will talk themselves out of doing new things. So the left brain overtakes the right brain. What I'm really pointing out here is that creativity is taking a generic offering and putting a twist on it to differentiate yourself. Being creative, or even zany—and zany is even farther out than creative—is a real challenge for most people, because only one in one hundred people is very creative. So if our listeners will just dedicate themselves to working on creativity, that means there will be two out of every hundred.

Let me just give the listeners and readers a few quick ideas which are a little bit "out there." Arrange for a mobile car washing company to arrive in your client's parking lot and wash every contact's vehicle. Friday is the best day because everybody likes a clean car on the weekend. So you'll get to earn the nickname "Mr. Clean" for taking somebody's business away in a sanitary manner.

Second one: arrange for a shoe shiner to set up a workstation at your client's office. Worried about being called a cobbler? I wouldn't, because that beats being called a peddler any day. Why do we always see shoeshine stands at the airport and hotels? Because that's where busy people are. So we want our competition to look at us as a heel because we took the shine off of them.

Next little one is stop giving Christmas gifts like everyone else does. It's best to give a gift on the first anniversary of the day when you first landed the client. Stop sending out Christmas cards in a mass way. We sit there and sign fifty or a hundred cards and there's no meaning to it. Instead, send a card today and you will get to monopolize the client's desk for a while.

Wright

Not to mention the fact that everyone is not a Christian.

Blades

Exactly. The last little one before we go to the next is one that I do a lot. I arrange for a masseuse to go to my clients' offices. They provide fifteen-minute chair massages. People stand in line for one. It looks like an opening for a blockbuster movie, because people are so stressed out these days. So a fifteen-minute stress-buster is a wonderful gift. Plus you hang around when the chief is getting his or her massage. Afterwards is the best time to ask for an order, because they are nice and relaxed and a bit groggy. You often get an answer back like, "Yeah, okay, whatever, sure."

Wright

Several years ago I was in the real estate business, and we were closing 1100 single-family dwellings a year, which in today's prices would be over a hundred million. I had a competitor that bought a truckload of pumpkins one Halloween and gave one to everyone in my subdivision of about six hundred houses. I hated him for years after that.

Blades

Good for him!

Wright

He literally captured most of the business in that entire neighborhood—with me living in it.

Blades

That's just doing the little things that other people don't do.

Wright

It seems to me that there have been more books written, more seminars and workshops held to teach employees about customer service than any other subject in the past ten years. Yet after all the training, customer service seems to be at an all-time low. How can that be?

Blades

Because most people talk about customer service. I help my clients to not just talk about good customer service; I get them to act on great client service. There's a big difference there in client service and customer service. Customers buy stuff. When you have a client relationship, where you give great client service, you're working on a long-term win-win. Check out your gift-giving ratio; that is, as a sales person, do you get more gifts from clients than you give out? That is a real stunner for a lot of people. If you have to pay for all the meals and the golfing, it means that your personal level of value-added services is way too low.

When I was in the corporate world, one of the things that I did for large potential clients was to provide them with complimentary sales training seminars, management consulting, seminars on exporting, when most of America didn't know how to do it that well, and many other programs, It was like pulling cherries off a tree, because they would often say, "Bill, this is absolutely fantastic! How am I going to pay you back?" Easy answer: "I would just like to have all your business." So good customer service is a must, but the salesperson has got to be thinking great client service.

Wright

What do you mean when you talk about proactive leadership? I would think that all leadership would have to be proactive, is it not?

Blades

The unfortunate part is that most aren't leaders. Most are still just managers. And most of the managers, who manage today, are managing the same way they were managed earlier in their career. They will only become leaders once they understand the huge difference. Let me give our listeners just a couple of things that fall under the realm of being proactive. Number one is culture. Leaders are the spearhead for the corporation's culture. You have to have a fanaticism with a great culture.

Number two is planning—being very proactive with a sales and marketing plan in the business plans where you meet or beat the deadline dates. I get my clients to pull their sales and marketing plan down off the shelf monthly, not when it's too late.

Number three is time utilization. Leaders need to be spending the majority of their time in two major areas—their own people, and then get out there with clients.

The fourth one is thinking. Leaders have got to take the necessary quiet time. I call it "day at the pond" or "day with the ducks"—taking time alone to just think. Currently, I have four retainer clients from across the U.S. and Canada. In three of those cases, I work with the president and VP of sales. I want them to visit me, not me going there. And we take the quiet time to relax a little bit and get on the golf course. I want them here where they are away from all the stresses and strains and we all can put our number one attribute together, our brains.

Next one is feedback. Leaders need to be asking their people and clients all the time, "What can I do better to serve you? What help do you need?"

Next one is failing. Leaders need to encourage their people to fail more than they have ever done before. When they're failing, it means they're doing new things.

Creativity. Encourage every single employee to put a creative idea on the table once a month. I get my clients to set up incentives for the creative ideas. Sometimes we give a reward for the person with the dumbest dud. The reason is that with a dud once in a while, you get the great ones.

Next one is appreciation. Leaders need to be giving appreciation to the people for doing great stuff. You cannot treat your people with indifference.

Next one is fun. Leaders understand that they must have the most fun place in town to work. Then, teamwork goes up, productivity goes up and, ultimately, sales go up.

The next area is giving. Leaders gain respect and power by sharing their time and talents and not taking credit from others.

Next is listening. Leaders ask tons of questions of other people and ask for the truth and listen to every word.

The next one is cutting edge. Leaders need to make sure that they are always working on new, unheard of services.

And succession. The president and all the VPs and managers must have a succession plan in place. Everyone must be trained and educated and ready to step up. Why do that? Because from the American Society of Training and Development, the latest number is eight-seven percent of all managers in the United States become managers without any previous training or education to get the job done.

Wright

They were probably the best salespeople in the company, and for that reason they were elevated to sales management.

Blades

That would be like taking Sammy Sosa off the baseball field and making him a manager.

Wright

When you took your company from thirteen million to thirty-three million in sales, did you create a "culture of greatness" that you teach other organizations?

Blades

Absolutely. I made it very tough to get on board. I was looking for the best of the best. And when I first started recruiting, I turned to some recruiters and said, "I do not want them from my industry. I don't even want them from any segment of the food industry. I want you to find me the best attitude and raw talent you can find." Then before I would bring a new salesperson on board, I would say, "I'm going to confirm this in writing, but I want you to hear me out. For one year, I don't even want to hear anything like, 'Gee, Bill, I wish we had this product to sell.' I want you to take what we have, listen to me, and run with it and create a track record where you will be famous out there. Then I'm going to embrace you with open arms, and I'm going to go get the new products you want." I wanted it tough to get on board, and I wanted to make sure the good and great ones were treated so well they wouldn't leave.

Wright

What is it about sales and salespeople that turns customers off?

Blades

Oh, boy! There are several biggies. One is don't be late. I show up thirty to forty minutes ahead of time because I plan on a traffic accident. I'm there thirty to forty minutes early. I take my trade magazine with me to read in the lobby. We've got our cell phones and laptops, and we can be working while waiting. Second one is don't exaggerate. I've told salespeople a million times, "Don't exaggerate."

The next kicker is that salespeople do not adjust their personal style to fit the client's style. They have one style and they think it's fine just like it is. Your clients will have one of four different personality styles, and you'd better find out which one before you ever walk in the door.

Wright

Did you do any personal profiling, such as the DISC or Myers-Briggs?

Blades

Always. Today, none of my clients bring any new sales and management people on without me profiling the candidates, and then I will use that profiling as an interview tool to really cut to the chase.

The next killer is salespeople drone on and on. That's a total waste of time, because, unfortunately, males only have a three-sentence attention span. The challenge is, they're not asking enough questions; they're just talking. They're not doing enough note taking. And the bottom line on your question is real selling is ninety percent asking great questions, listening intently to every single word, making meticulous notes, and only ten percent talking.

Wright

Years ago, I had a consulting service that helped hire people for companies. After researching it, we found that ninety percent of the time the person who was doing the interview did the talking, and the interviewee talked only ten percent of the time. We reminded them that maybe they should start listening and stop talking so much.

Blades

Right. It's a plague.

Wright

Bill, with our *Mission Possible!* talk show and book, we are trying to encourage people in our audience to be better, to live better and be more fulfilled by listening to the examples of our guests. Is there anyone or anything in your life that has made a difference for you and helped you to be a better person?

Blades

Two people. One of my role models is Clebe McClary. He wanted the Marine Corps, he wanted his second lieutenant bars, he wanted the infantry, he wanted Vietnam, and he got all four wishes. But in reading his books and meeting him in a VA hospital, I found that he gave every ounce of himself to take care of his men. So I would suggest that our listeners and readers also go buy Clebe McClary's book.

Another good role model that I had in my life was at my last corporate job. The president had very strong Christian beliefs. There were several things that I observed. He walked his talk one hundred percent of the time. Secondly, he genuinely cared for his people and, thirdly, his ethics were the foundation of any business decision that was made. If it wasn't right, fair, aboveboard, we didn't do it. So, again, both of these men were not only role models, they were great leaders. They set a great example for everybody.

Wright

I've known Clebe for many years. He was in our town a couple of years ago. His entire family is as motivating as he is.

What do you think makes up a great mentor? In other words, are there characteristics that mentors seem to have in common?

Blades

I'm going to say there are mentors, and there are good and great mentors, just like there are speakers and consultants and then you have the good and great ones. Number one, they must have made the trip, that is, they must possess a very successful background.

Number two, they must tell the truth. If they're mentoring with an individual and they don't tell the truth, they're not helping them; they're actually hurting them. I find that most managers and leaders hold back on telling the truth because they're afraid it might hurt their feelings. But what they're doing is hurting them.

Third one for a mentor: they must really care about the person. It's not our job to mentor for money. Our real job is to serve as a mentor to help people. I speak about fifty times a year. It used to be eighty, but I cut back so I could do more consulting, and now I consult about a hundred and fifty days a year. I enjoy the consulting and mentoring much more because I get to help people one at a time. And I get to monitor and watch them grow, so for me it's personally more rewarding than getting up and speaking at a convention where I don't have a clue what happens after I leave.

Wright

The monitoring part is really the rewarding part isn't it?

Blades

Exactly

Wright

You served as the finance chairman for Newt Gingrich. Obviously, you were around politicians who were about as high as you can get on the political ladder. Do you feel that politicians in our country are fair and honest or are they doing things for their own parties?

Blades

I think you have good ones and bad ones. When I initially served as Newt Gingrich's financial chairman, there had not been a Republican senator or representative elected in the state of Georgia since the Civil War. We had a real challenge on our hands. We met the challenge, but I think a lot of our leaders get up in Washington and they start to believe their own press clippings. So I am a strong proponent that the best role models in this country are almost always found in the business world.

Wright

I have been in some political campaigns and helped out in several different positions. To me, compromise doesn't mean meeting halfway; it means giving up what you believe in so that maybe the next time around you can get what you believe in. I just don't think I could do that.

Blades

Leaders need convictions and to stick to them.

Wright

When you consider the choices you have made down through the years, has faith played an important role in your life?

Blades

David, in two different areas: number one, faith in myself. At my last corporate job in Tennessee, I was about to be named president. I was making a very comfortable living, but I wanted to pursue my love, which is training and education. So I cut the cord, went out on my own, and in the first year I made far less than one-half of my last year in corporate life. I didn't have any doubt then as to the outcome. In the second year, I more than doubled my salary and bonus in the corporate world. I just knew year one would be tough, but I wanted to follow something that I felt I was very good at, so I had faith in myself; I had faith on how it would work out.

Now the second one: I don't pray very often, and I have hardly ever prayed for myself; but a couple of years ago, I was doing a tremendous amount of traveling, and while I was away, I found out that I had been embezzled. I prayed for myself, probably for the first time in five to ten years. I just said, "If it's right for me, please help me." I didn't say, "I need your help." It was amazing. My business went through the roof for the next eighteen months. It was like my telephone had a magnet on it. So the eighteen months after I prayed were the best eighteen months in the sixteen years I've been speaking and consulting. Amazing.

Wright

That is amazing.

Most people are fascinated with the new TV shows about being a survivor. What has been the greatest comeback you have made from adversity in your career or life?

Blades

I'm going to give an example out of the speaking and consulting career. I started my small business in Tennessee in the late eighties, and I moved the business to Arizona. I had lived here before and loved it. On the business side, there are a tremendous amount of conventions that come to Phoenix, so I would get to speak for a lot of conventions and go home and sleep in my own bed.

But then three challenges hit within the first year of my moving. The recession hit and we had the Gulf War. People were canceling meetings; they didn't want their people on airplanes. But then the potential death knock came at the door. We were going to have a vote on whether to have a Martin Luther King holiday or not. It was going to pass, but the commissioner of the National Football League came to Phoenix and told the voters that "if you don't pass the Martin Luther King holiday, we're going to pull the Super Bowl away from you." Well, people in Arizona didn't like that threat, so they voted in the negative. It got 49.9% of the vote, but there was over a ten percent swing in voters.

When the Super Bowl was pulled, associations also pulled their conventions out of Arizona. My business was going down quickly. The fallout among speakers and consultants was tremendous. So I added two full-time sales people. I went from a five-cent brochure to a brochure that literally cost a dollar and five cents. Phone bills went through the roof, marketing materials went through the roof, and postage went through the roof; but the result was that by refusing to participate in the recession, we had a fantastic year. I had the adversity, and I could either elect to go along with the recession and use it as an excuse, or buck up and do what I tell my clients to do: when times are tough, get tougher and get going.

Wright

Let me ask you a question about the CMC designation. I know it's a certification by the Institute of Management Consultants and, of course, it's a mark of excellence. But you are one out of sixteen internationally who speak and consult with clients in area of sales management?

Blades

That's correct.

Wright

My goodness! What did it take to get that?

Blades

First, just the very basic thing: you have to be a consultant for three years. Then, you have to take the written and oral exams and re-exams. Now, there are only one thousand certified management consultants in all fields internationally. Most consultants are like most sales and management people—they think they're fine just like they are. On the other hand, the Institute of Management Consultants is very exacting, which meant that I wanted to be part of the Institute of Management Consultants and get my certification. They also evaluate your previous engagements by talking to your past clients.

Wright

I was reading one of your presentations, "Re-energizing the Organization for Greatness." It can't be just skills training, can it? Almost every corporation does skills training. What makes yours different, that it would be an energizing force? Also the word "greatness" is rarely heard in corporate language.

Blades

In all of my clients' buildings, you hear the word "greatness" because I let it be known on the first day I go in as consultant that greatness is what we're going for. But I let them know in oral and written form that the only way I will take the assignment is if I have one hundred percent commitment from them in certain areas. Now let me spell that out: culture. It will be a culture of greatness from everybody; and if anyone does not want to participate, we invite them to go to another team.

Wright

We are out of time. I could sit and talk to you all day long.

Today we have been talking to Bill Blades who is a professional speaker, trainer, consultant, and author—and, as we have learned, a very interesting person. Bill Blades, thank you for joining us on _Mission Possible!_

Blades

Thank you for having me. It was my pleasure.

William Blades, LLC
25555 N. Windy Walk Dr. #55
Scottsdale, AZ 85255
(480) 563-5355
E-mail: bill@williamblades.com
www.williamblades.com

Chapter 11

Tom Hopkins

Tom Hopkins, Founder of Tom Hopkins International, is widely accepted as one of the world's premier sales trainers and motivators. He is in great demand as a speaker. His books are sold worldwide and include Low Profile Selling: Act Like a Lamb, Sell Like a Lion; Your Guide to Greatness in Sales; The Official Guide to Success; *and* Sales Prospecting for Dummies.

The Interview

David Wright (Wright)

Tom Hopkins is a sales legend. The basis of Tom's training is how-to strategies and tactics, not motivational hype. Due to the extraordinary demand for the unique training he offers, Tom has received international recognition and earned a reputation that is synonymous with effectiveness, productivity, and integrity. His material transcends a wide variety of cultures and has been translated into eleven foreign languages. His live seminars have been presented in North America, Europe, Africa, Asia, and Australia. Tom's credibility lies in his track record and the track records of the students he has trained over the years. He has personally trained over three million students on five continents. He has shared the stage with some of the greatest men of our times, including retired General Schwarzkopf, former President George Bush and Barbara Bush, General Colin Powell, and Lady Margaret Thatcher. Tom has authored eight books, including *How to Master the Art of Selling* and *Selling for Dummies.* His first book, *How to Master the Art of Selling,* has sold over 1.3 million copies and has been translated into ten languages. It is used as a textbook in sales and marketing classes and is required reading for new sales people by many sales and management professionals in a wide variety of industries. Tom's latest book is entitled *Sell It Today, Sell It Now: Mastering the Art of the One-Call Close.* Tom Hopkins, welcome to *Mission Possible!*

Tom Hopkins (Hopkins)

Well, thank you; it's nice to be back on the program.

Wright

Tom, today I'd like to talk about your latest book; however, I don't want to miss the opportunity to ask you some questions that I think might help our readers and listeners in many areas of their lives. In an article titled "First Impression," you wrote that a person is judged in the first fifteen to twenty seconds when they first meet someone. Is that really true?

Hopkins

Yes. In fact, we live in a very judgmental society, and when someone looks at you, they start judging you. Now maybe not on a conscious level, but subconsciously they are evaluating the way they feel about your look and how you're dressed. That's why you smile when you first meet people. That's why you dress appropriately, depending on who you are going to be with and where you are going. If I were going to a seminar, I would wear a full suit and, oftentimes, cufflinks, because I would feel totally dressed up. Because I'm an instructor, I would want to present an appropriate visual message. So people do judge in fifteen seconds the way you come across, your face, your dress, and, of course, the words you say.

Wright

In the article you went on to say that there are several ways a person could create a favorable impression. Can you give us a few things that we can do?

Hopkins

Sure. First of all, be genuinely happy when you first meet people. They'll mirror back how you come across when you meet them. So the smile is very important. I've always joked that if you look like you're weaned on a pickle, then I don't want a long-term relationship with you. So you smile and always give them good eye contact. Many people have a belief that "If you don't look at me, then I can't trust you." Now I don't believe that's true; but if they do, it is. So you give them good eye contact. Also, I feel that the handshake is important; if you are going to shake their hand, it should be deep, in a firm grip. People judge your confidence level by the handshake that you have. Those are just a few concepts. Also, remembering names is so important. Lots of people are introduced to somebody, and they're so nervous about the first-time meeting they forget the person's name. So I ask my students to repeat names four times, and it's amazing how they will stick—of course, repeat them to yourself when you do that.

Wright

I was interested in what you said about mirroring. Do people generally do what you do?

Hopkins

Well, no. What I meant by that was, I feel that if they have a certain demeanor, you want to try and match their demeanor. But I know if I walked up to you and I had a very angry or sullen look, you are not going to come back at me with a real warm look. So again, they do, in a way, come back at you the way you come at them. The warmth and the smile and all that are very important.

Wright

In another article you wrote for publication, titled "How to Handle an Angry Client," you gave some great advice that offered a nine-step technique that you have developed. Can you describe some of the ways that you dispel anger in your clients?

Hopkins

Sure. Many times today people lose their temper. We're in a very high-stress, high-anxiety society. You can't make everybody happy. You need to learn certain sentences like "I understand how you feel" or "John, I can appreciate your feelings" or "John, I can't agree with you more; we did make a mistake here." Agree with the adversaries instead of fighting them. If you have an angry client, don't be afraid to apologize. I have clients call me up—I was in the real estate business, and the interest rates went up. It wasn't my fault, but suddenly they'd call and say, "Tom, it's a quarter percent more than you said it was going to be." I would always say, "First of all, John, I understand how you feel. I'm sure you're aware I can't control the prime interest rate." And then of course I'd also say, "Let me make a few notes of what we talked about. Now back when we talked two and a half months ago, the interest rates were this, and that's what I told you, right?" and everything was fine.

Another thing, David, is that people should slow the client down when they're angry. For example, I'd have an angry client, and I'd say, "I'm going to document this in writing so I don't forget the things you're upset about, so let's go over that again now." You are happy with this, and you see that people just like to feel they are being heard, listened to. Too many people feel that if they are angry and you come back at that, they've got to fight; and you can never win an argument with a client—it's just part of sales. You have to learn to apologize. Make notes of their concerns. Let them know you are doing your best to serve them. I've always found that if you humble yourself and come back with a real nice feeling, that will usually offset much of their anger.

Wright

I was fascinated by a statement you made in an article titled "Knowing When to Close." You wrote that many salespeople get so wrapped up in their selling sequence that if the client wants it before they are through presenting, they won't even let them have it. So, how do you know when it's time to close a transaction?

Hopkins

I've got to level with you. This subject you just asked me about would take two and a half hours at full speed to cover, so I'm going to give you just a couple concepts. First of all, what I meant was, many people in sales love their product; and after they really learn their presentation, they almost feel like the client has to hear everything before they are even ready to purchase. Now many buyers are not that way. The buyer may decide that he has a need for the product, and it financially makes sense. To many of them, time is precious, and they want the darn product, so they'll ask the right type of questions, like suddenly they'll stop the person showing the vehicle or showing the home, and say, "Look, how soon can we get this product?" or "How soon can we have it delivered?" People don't ask that question unless there is sincere buying interest. Of course, the average person in sales misses that; but I know that if I were showing you a home and you said to me, "Look, how soon can we take possession if everything else makes sense on this home?" I know that's a buying question, so I say, "I think the seller is somewhat flexible. What would best suit you if everything else makes sense?" He says, "We'd like to try to get in by summer," and I'd say, "That's about a forty-five day closing; does that sound about right to you?" "Well, yeah, that sounds about right." "Why don't we go ahead?" And right then is when I'm going to draft up our thoughts on the purchase agreement.

Wright

Right.

Hopkins

So the time to close is when the buyer either asks you the right questions or you see them getting a little fidgety. It's time for you to ask a very simple question. "John, how are you feeling about all this so far?" You ask them that question, and they say, "You know I feel pretty good, and it's something we should probably do." Well, you're done presenting; you've done all you should do. Now you say, "Why don't we just draft up our feelings and see how it looks on paper?" And then you ask them for their middle initial. "John, do you have a middle initial?" He says, "B." And you write it up on the paperwork, "John B. Johnson," and away you go.

Wright

You're saying that salespeople just miss buying signals?

Hopkins

All too often the buyer wants it before they're willing to let them have it. I watch this so often.

Wright

Tom, let's talk about your latest book, *Sell It Today, Sell it Now: Mastering the Art of the One-Call Close.* I was in real estate for several years, and I had to show my prospects several homes before I finally sold them. Would this book help me reduce the time it takes to sell clients?

Hopkins

Oh, yes. That's the main reason I wrote the book. You'll notice the book isn't called "Mastering the Art of the One-Time Close." It's the *One-Call Close,* meaning that on this particular call—let's say, you came into my office looking for a home. And you said, "We're in no hurry," as everyone says. Then I take you out on a Saturday and I show you different homes, watching for buying signs; and sure enough, I hit a home that makes sense. You give me the right buying signs, and you are qualified for it. Well, I go back to the office to outline all the financial aspects. My goal is that before you leave, I'm going to close that transaction. Now there are numerous things you say and do; this is an hour-and-a-half process.

But now let's say, for example, I take you out on Saturday; you're a very finicky buyer. I cannot seem to find the right house.

Well, my closing this time is to say that I'm going to go out this week and scour the inventory. I'm going to look at all the homes the other brokers have, and by next Saturday or Sunday I'm confident I'll have the right home. I want a commitment to come back, so that's why I use that particular closing—it's the one-call close. Now there are a lot of salespeople who go into a home and market a home improvement of some type; but when they give the buyer all the information they need, they had better go into a final closing sequence and get the check, or they'll probably never hear from the people again. They'll buy from someone else.

Wright

I sat through a condominium project closing situation last week. Once in a while I do it just to sharpen my sales skills. Not only was I turned over twice to someone higher, my wife and I counted twenty-seven closing attempts. Unbelievable! They were very good.

Hopkins

Well, many of the people in that industry have to be very good, because that is a difficult closing. But if they have a good product and you're qualified, they sure have a right to attempt to close it.

Wright

It just so happened that I needed it, so I bought it.

Hopkins

That's always the way it is, David; I'm the easiest one to sell myself.

Wright

In the book you talk about the four levels of competency—of the salesperson, I imagine. Would you tell us what they are?

Hopkins

Sure. In fact, these apply to any industry, any job, any sport. The first level is what we call the *unconscious incompetent*. This is when a person starts to do something like, let's say, get into sales. They don't even know they don't know. They just know that people say, "You get along well with people; you would be good in sales." I call them unconscious and incompetent. They don't even know what they are doing in sales.

Level two is called the *conscious incompetent*. They've been in sales three weeks. Rejected every day, they've made no money. Now they consciously realize they don't know what the heck they are doing, so they become consciously incompetent.

Then they rise to the next level—let's say they go to a seminar, they read a book, or they go to training; and all of a sudden, a month later, they become *consciously competent*. That's the third level. Now conscious, competent salespeople have to think about what they are doing. They don't operate on a reflex. They go to a presentation with notes. Then they start making some money, because they finally learned the company presentation. The money starts to come in, and all of a sudden they get excited. They get more training. They get the biggest income month ever. They stay in sales the next three to five years and they don't even think about what they do. They know what to say on the telephone.

They now rise to the fourth level of competency, which is called the *unconscious competent*. That means they unconsciously function. They don't even have to think; everything they do is a total reflex. If the buyer says he wants to think it over, they know exactly what to say. If the buyer says it costs too much, they know exactly what to say. That's the four levels salespeople go through, as far as competencies.

Wright

Is the fourth level the same as internalization?

Hopkins

Yes, it is. It's someone that's totally internalized what to say and do, and they just operate almost on a reflex. They don't even think any more. That's the highest paid people; they're tops in the industry.

Wright

In your book you also point to four concepts that control all sales. Would you share those with us?

Hopkins

The first concept is that the potential buyer has to have a need, and you've got to be sure that they do by asking the right questions. They have to be qualified, which means that they can financially purchase the product or service. Then, of course, I feel that you have to see the desire level increase as you present. The fourth thing that you have to have is that they are ready to make a decision if everything fits into place. Now, there are people who can't make the decision because they are not the decision maker. So there's no way to close. We call that a "condition"—they're not even the right person, but that controls the sale.

Wright

You know, the qualification process, to a lot of people, seems as if it's cut and dried; but I remember several years ago, a new fellow who worked for me in the real estate business showed a couple some houses they could not afford. Obviously, they fell in love with one of them. I told him if a person can only qualify for a one hundred thousand dollar house, don't show several two hundred thousand dollar houses. Of course they're going to want them.

Hopkins

Oh, it's a big mistake. Salespeople ruin the buyer by showing them things that, sure, they love, but they just don't have the financial capacity to afford them.

Wright

The lady came into my office and actually cried, so I spent the next day apologizing to both her and her husband.

Hopkins

Sure. It must have been difficult.

Wright

Tom, you spend a lot of time in your book on the subject of overcoming objections, so it must be important. You made a suggestion that a salesperson should let the customers answer their own objections. How does that happen?

Hopkins

Well, first of all, it comes back to one major art form, and that's questioning. It's a basic concept that most people in the United States want to own lots of things. It will make their life happier, better, safer, more secure, whatever; but they are afraid to buy until they do a couple of things. First of all, they can't say yes until they give you some type of no. I learned over the years that the toughest sale to make is to the buyer that likes everything, with no objections whatsoever. So the real pro says, "I've got to hear the no before I overcome that to get the yes." Also, I feel that by asking the right questions they can answer their own objections. For example, let's say we walk into a bedroom of a home we're showing; I can tell the wife likes everything, but the husband says, "I think this bedroom for the kids is just too small." Well, all I'm going to do is feed that back to him: "Now, John, your concern is the size of this third bedroom; is that what's bothering you right now?" And he'll say, "Well, yeah, it is." And the wife likes everything else. She'll start answering the objection for you. She'll start saying things like, "Honey, I love the rest of the house. The kids are only going to be with us another few years. We're going to probably be here the rest of our lives." So I just sit back and let her handle it, and the process of handling objections is—I would call it a very, very serious concept you have to learn.

One of the keys is people don't object unless they have a desire, so by understanding the objection you can then plan the strategy to overcome it. If they say to me, "Tom, I feel it costs too much" – well, I look at that as something good, because people don't fight the investment unless there is interest to own it. So when someone says to me, "It costs too much," inside I say, "Hot dog! There's interest here!" I just smile and say, "You know, John, today most things seem to cost too much." So I get him to give me a figure. When I have that figure, I now know what I need to overcome the money objection.

Wright

You know, when many people think of sales as a career, they are filled with terror. Do you think that most great salespeople are born with natural ability to succeed, or can almost anyone develop the skills necessary to become successful?

Hopkins

This is something I've fought for years. There are some people in sales who totally believe that they're naturals, and if they are naturals, they don't need training. On the other hand, the people who aren't really feeling they're a natural are going to be afraid they can't do it. I believe that people who are "naturals" usually are too talkative, too overbearing, too much like a salesperson, whereas the person who's kind of timid, shy, and afraid can do really well if they learn the profession and go through training.

If we look at two temperaments, or personalities, the first is the *interested introvert,* a very shy, somewhat timid person. The opposite is the *interesting extrovert,* the outgoing, aggressive, somewhat controlling personality. I believe that the interesting extrovert is too much like a salesperson and threatens people, whereas the interested introvert is very interested in people. They can do extremely well, because they are willing to give up control of the conversation. They're better listeners. They care more about the feelings of the other person. So these are all things I think people have to evaluate when they look at selling.

Wright

Tom, I have used your sales training for many years, mostly through audio cassettes. I formed the habit years ago of listening to training tapes when I'm in my car. It seems that your book *Sell It Today, Sell It Now: Mastering the Art of the One-Call Close* should be available on cassette tapes and CDs.

Hopkins

You know, we just finished it. I did a program just last month where I took the book and made a seminar out of it, because I'm like you—I don't have the time to sit down and read nearly as much as I should. So rather than try to read, I believe in cassettes or CDs, which we put this program on. People can take advantage of their driving time as learning time, and they're sure welcome to call my office if they'd like to get one of the first copies of that new program.

Wright

Great; if you'll give us the telephone number . . .

Hopkins

Well sure! They can find out about all of our products, everything we do, at 1-800-528-0446. Or if they'd like to, they can log on to our website. And one thing I do, David, is a new electronic newsletter, which comes out every month. There's no charge for it; it's complimentary. It gives the "Close of the Month," where we try every month to come up with something brand new for salespeople to use that month. People can get the newsletter if they will just log on to www.TomHopkins.com. They'll see everything we do. We have a whole menu of our products and services there.

Wright

Great. I know our listeners, as well as our readers, are going to love that. Tom, if you could have a platform and tell our audience something that would help or encourage them, what would you say?

Hopkins

I would say that, first of all, in a world that seems to take you off course and mess up your focus, I think people have to really work on setting their goals and committing to them. I believe goal setting is a key to success. People need to write down their long-term goals, what they want to accomplish in twenty years, then back off ten years, and five years, like a life blueprint. I believe that people should become goal-oriented and stay focused and surround themselves with positive people. If you listen to negativity, it's going to affect you emotionally. So I, of course, have a little saying: Don't take advice from anyone more messed up than you are. I totally believe we need to take those words into consideration in our lives. I just hope everyone realizes that we live in the greatest country in the world; we have the most wonderful opportunities, but people not only have to have knowledge about their profession but they have to focus on their goals. So, everybody, sit down with a piece of paper and draft up where you're going; because if you don't know where you're going, you're certainly going to end up somewhere else.

Wright

Tom, I've never gotten anything but great advice from you. Many, many years back, without even knowing it, you helped me build a real estate company that was closing eleven hundred single-family dwellings a year. That would be over a hundred million today.

Hopkins

Wow! Oh man, I didn't even know that, David! Thank you!

Wright

You were very helpful; I was buying everything that you had, and I really appreciate it. It's one of those cases where you don't know your mentors personally, but I respect you as one of my mentors.

Hopkins

Well, I thank you for that. It's always nice to be on your program, and I wish you all the best. And thank you all for listening today.

Wright

We have been talking to Tom Hopkins, who is truly a sales legend. Thank you so much for being with us today, Tom.

Hopkins

Thank you, David; I wish you all the best.

Tom Hopkins International

7531 East Second Street

Scottsdale, AZ 85251 USA

(480) 949-0786 or (800) 528-0446

Fax: (480) 949-1590

www.tomhopkins.com

Chapter 12

Steve Gilliland

Steve Gilliland is the CEO of Performance Plus, a Pittsburgh, Pennsylvania, based company dedicated to training and developing people worldwide. He is represented by the Washington Speakers Bureau, the most prestigious speakers bureau in the world.

The Interview

David E. Wright (Wright)

Today we are talking to Steve Gilliland, founder and CEO of Performance Plus, a company dedicated to training, developing, and improving people worldwide. His colorful background includes major league baseball, broadcasting, and eleven years of corporate management. Steve's clients include General Motors, CBS, Hilton Hotels, SmithKline Beecham, and the United States Marine Corps. He is a member of the American Society for Training and Development, the National Speakers Association and is represented by the prestigious Washington Speakers Bureau. Steve Gilliland, welcome to *Mission Possible!*

Steve Gilliland *(Gilliland)*

Thank you for the opportunity.

Wright

Steve, recently I was reading some of your company's material and came across something you said about attitude. Let me read it to you in part. "My attitude is either my best friend or my worst enemy. . . . It is the librarian of my past, the speaker of my present, and the prophet of my future." Do you really attach that much importance to attitude?

Gilliland

I do. Talent determines what you can do; motivation determines if you are willing to do it; but your attitude is going to determine how well you do it. I see a lot of people go through life with a lot of talent; however, they seem to squander it because they can't put all the pieces together. The old cliché that attitude is everything, I totally believe that. Maybe the single biggest indicator of our attitude is adversity. The remarkable part of life is that we all have a choice when it comes to our attitude and outlook on life. People blame so much of their attitude on circumstances without taking responsibility for how they react to them. Fumbles are a part of football, failing is a part of succeeding, and hurting is a part of loving. Every situation in life is our perception of it, not the reality of it. The glass is half empty or half full, and sometimes our perception will be based on whether we're pouring or drinking. When our attitudes outdistance our abilities, the impossible becomes possible.

Wright

Dennis Brown says the difference between a good day and a bad day is your attitude. I think he might be right. I was watching a video of a presentation you made to a large corporate audience, and you were talking about life being a "trip" and that everyone should enjoy the ride. More specifically, you were telling people to "cure your destination disease." What's that all about?

Gilliland

Robert Hastings wrote an essay entitled "The Station," in which he said, "Tucked away in our subconscious is an idyllic vision. We see ourselves on a long trip that spans the continent. We are traveling by train. Out the window we drink in the passing scene of cars on nearby highways, of children waving at a crossing, of cattle grazing on a distant hillside, of smoke pouring from a power plant, of row upon row of corn and wheat, of flatlands and valleys, of mountains and rolling hillsides, of city skylines and village halls. But uppermost in our minds is the final destination. On a certain day, at a certain hour, we will pull into the station. Bands will be playing and flags waving. Once we get there, so many wonderful dreams will come true and the pieces of our lives will fit together like a completed jigsaw puzzle. How restlessly we pace the aisles. Damning the minutes for loitering—waiting, waiting, waiting for the station. 'When we reach the station, that will be it!' we cry. 'When I'm 18 . . . when I buy a new 450 SL Mercedes Benz . . . when I put the last kid through college . . . pay off the mortgage . . . when I get a promotion . . . when I reach the age of retirement, then I shall live happily ever after!' Sooner or later we must realize there is no station, no one place to arrive at, once and for all. The true joy of life is the trip. The station is only a dream. It constantly outdistances us."

I got to thinking how true this was. We all have this destination disease. During the times when I was most successful I never got a chance to truly enjoy it because I was always thinking about what I was going to do next. I caught myself a couple of years ago living my life fifteen minutes ahead every day and decided to start enjoying each moment. My advice to people is simple: take more walks, go barefoot more often, watch more sunsets, eat more ice cream (chocolate chip cookie dough), dance more, laugh more, and cry less. Stop pacing the aisles, counting the miles, and watching the clock. The final destination will come soon enough. Enjoy the ride!

Wright

That's great advice. Steve, you talk a lot about integrity. In view of the things that have happened recently in corporations that have put their stockholders at risk by their decisions, how does one learn how to succeed without compromise?

Gilliland

By doing the right thing, at the right time, for the right reason. Too many times when we are faced with a choice between what is best and what is right, we choose what is best. I always challenge people to make sure as they climb the ladder of success that it is leaning against the right wall. A good rule to follow is always making sure that your actions match your beliefs. We try to teach values, when in reality we should realize that values are not taught, values are caught. Actually the word integrity is an interesting word defined in different ways by different people to fit different circumstances. If you look it up in the dictionary, the word that always jumps out is consistency. With that in mind, we must learn to be consistent in our thoughts, actions, and habits, which inevitably add up to our character.

Wright

I have found that the right way generally works out the best.

Gilliland

Absolutely.

Wright

I have heard it said that nothing is consistent except change. Since you teach people to embrace change and interpret change as opportunity, do you have any tips that will make change easier for us?

Gilliland

Stay alert. When you become comfortable, you sometimes are not aware of what is happening, and you begin to take things for granted. The key is to always remind yourself that change is inevitable; however, growth is optional. Ironically, our growth is many times determined by how fast we can recognize change and actually respond to it. My advice to people is to always expect problems, changes and choices to be ongoing. If you anticipate change, you can handle it . . . and if you don't, you can become extinct. In addition, I have personally realized that the sooner we can let go of our past, the sooner we can realize our future. We all need to live more for today, less for tomorrow, and never about yesterday. Yesterday is filled with regret and resentment, twin thieves that rob us of our potential and prohibit us from embracing change. We constantly let people and circumstances that are beyond our control rent space in our minds. The sooner we focus on what we can control, and realize, most of all, that we can't even control the speed of change, the easier our lives will be.

Wright

I remember many years ago reading *Future Shock* by Alvin Tofler, and he kept saying it is not change as much as it is the rate of change. I know what he was talking about now that I've gotten a little bit older. I get so much information in a day's time, it's almost as if I'm sitting in front of a fire hydrant and information is coming out of the fire hydrant like water at full pressure and I'm drinking with a straw. I just seem to miss most of everything that is going by me. If there was any way that change could be embraced, I think it would help our audience a lot to understand that change is so rapid that nobody can get it all.

Gilliland

It's ironic that many of us grew up learning the Serenity Prayer, even memorizing it, and yet we have never learned to live by it: "God grant me the serenity to accept the things I cannot change, the courage to change the things I can, and the wisdom to know the difference." Think about it—it's not the changes that stress us out, it's our inability to quickly recognize where our role is in the whole change process. Every change in our life, whether it is personal or professional, comes down to accepting our role and then moving beyond it. There is an old saying that says, "If you don't like what you're getting, change what you're doing." Interpretation: If you always do what you've always done, you always get what you always do.

Wright

I heard someone say that you believe in teaching people to do ordinary things in an extraordinary way. Can you tell us how you do that?

Gilliland

Passion, energy, and enthusiasm. These three combined can turn the ordinary into the extraordinaryy. I define passion as loving what you do, loving why you do it, and loving who you do it with. I recently asked a group of hospital employees this question: If every job in the world paid the same, where would you work?

Wright

That's a great question.

Gilliland

The main reason I ask it is to challenge them to check their passion. If they forget why they do what they do, then they lose an important ingredient in being passionate. Loving what you do is important; however, when you forget why you do it, then you've taken a step backwards and just made it ordinary. To be extraordinary takes energy, and some people lack the recipe for energy—sleep, diet, and exercise. A gentleman asked me one time, "How do you get up so early?" To which I respond, "I go to bed." In order to put the "extra" in ordinary, you have to have the energy to do it. People who eat right, sleep right, and exercise have always had an advantage over those people who don't.

For years I, too, wanted to achieve so many things; however, I wasn't willing to make the sacrifice—or should I say choice—to change my approach to how I did things. Creating Your Edge™ is a mindset that allows you to realize that every advantage in life is created by a choice. Most accomplishments are a result of relentless effort that takes persistency that is driven by energy. In the process, it is imperative that you never lose your enthusiasm for what you do. To never lose your enthusiasm you have to maintain your positive outlook, your sense of humor, and at times do whatever it takes —WIT. I'm always reminded of my son who delivered pizza, a pretty ordinary job to many; however, he created his edge and made it extraordinary. He loved what he did, understood why he did it (the importance), and thoroughly enjoyed all the new people he met while making deliveries. He met all the requirements of sleep, diet and exercise, which made him energetic and willing to make deliveries, while some of the delivery personnel opted to let him go while they stayed behind to play arcade games. His enthusiasm and "Whatever It Takes" approach made him enjoy the job even more and earn three times the tips the other delivery personnel made. His largest tip was twenty dollars from a guy who didn't want the free liter of Pepsi with his large pizza because he only liked Coke. My son stopped by a convenience store, purchased a liter of Coke from his tip money, and promptly delivered the pizza and Coke. The gentleman was so astonished by what he had done he handed him thirty dollars and told him to keep the change, a perfect example of "Creating Your Edge" and turning the ordinary into the extraordinary, or shall we say WIT—Whatever It Takes!

Wright

That's right. You have said that goal setting, focus, and commitment are behind most successful people. In a fast-paced society, it is getting more difficult to implement these three principles. Can you help our audience and readers understand how to go about it?

Gilliland

It's hard to imagine getting on an airplane and the pilot giving the announcements and saying something like this: "Folks, we're glad you chose this flight, and we're going to do everything we can to get you to your destination. We don't have a flight plan and aren't really sure when we'll arrive, if we even do arrive, but don't worry; should we not get you where you wanted to go, then please try us tomorrow and we'll give it another whirl." You would think they were nuts. So look at us. We get up some days with no plan, no deadline, no target, and when the day ends we are frustrated we didn't get somewhere. Most people I have met who aren't sure where they are headed end up arriving where they planned to end up—nowhere! I measure success by what we finish, not by what we start. Too often people list out their goals; however, they never have a plan to achieve them, a deadline to finish them, and most importantly, a persistence to stay focused on them. They try to do too much and end up failing. Someone once said, "Improve one hundred things one percent, instead of one thing one hundred percent." Oops, did I just say "sweat the small stuff"? In essence, what I am saying is that if we break the goals into small chunks, we will stay energized, because we will get excited about our small successes. Another perspective is that we need to appreciate what we have, where we are, and enjoy the process of getting there.

Earlier in this interview I mentioned that we all have this destination disease. People who are goal setters tend to have the disease and live too far ahead instead of enjoying the moment. Solution: plan the future but stay focused in the present. Paul McCartney of the Beatles said they never truly enjoyed their success because they were always too busy planning what was next. Goal setting is not for the purpose of what's next, it's for the purpose of where you are heading. Commitment is "no-matter-what," while focus allows us to enjoy what we are doing at the time. Appreciate the process, and the achievement will be even sweeter. You mentioned that we live in a fast-paced society, which we do; however, as I mentioned earlier, the true joy of life is in the trip.

Know where you're headed; take small steps to get there; don't let anyone or anything stop you; keep focused on what you're doing so you can appreciate the process.

Wright

I agree with the "small chunk" theory. With our *Mission Possible!* talk show and book we are trying to encourage people in our audience to be better, live better, and be more fulfilled by listening to the examples of our guests. Is there anyone or anything in your life that has made a difference for you and helped you be a better person?

Gilliland

Yes, David, there have been a lot of people that have influenced my life, including a former secretary, Margaret Shannon; a great mom, Pat Wise; and an incredible wife, Charlotte. I tease my mom; many times I'll introduce her to an audience, even though she isn't there, by saying, "My mom is a King James Version, front-row, Bible-slinging, fundamental, fire-breathing Baptist. Her prayers and persistence on her knees had a great influence on me accepting Jesus Christ as my personal savior.

But I'd have to say the most influential person in my life and the one who has helped me to make the biggest changes is my wife, Charlotte. She is the one who has kept me grounded. She's the one who has kept me focused. She is the person who, when we come to the fork in the road, is always turning right and making sure I do the right things, at the right time, for the right reason. She is just a very ethical and honest person. That's not to say that I'm not, but sometimes you can tend to rationalize your behavior, and it doesn't match your actions to your beliefs. For example, you're traveling and they cancel your flight, or you're late or delayed and your reaction isn't exemplary of what you believe. She is always there to give me the balance in my life, the voice of reason to help me through every situation. The other thing she has done is teach me to put a value on circumstances. As she reminds me, "If you are going to be a speaker, if you're going to be an author, the greatest testimony you will ever have is that your actions match your beliefs." She is probably the greatest leader I know. She is an incredible daughter, sister, mother, and wife. When they pass out awards for being a great person, my wife, Charlotte, will win in every category.

Wright

Great examples, especially your mother. Even though it's a humorous comment, it's probably all true.

Gilliland

She's a keeper.

Wright

Someone asked me why I went to church every Sunday. Was it because God would do something to me when I get to heaven if I didn't? I tell them that I'm not worried about God. I have to pass my mother before I get to him, and you don't want to know what she would do to me for laying out of church.

Gilliland

That's right. I told somebody one time that my mom had the toll-free number to heaven a long time before I had that toll-free number to my business.

Wright

What do you think makes up a great mentor? In other words, are there characteristics that mentors seem to have in common?

Gilliland

One characteristic would be patience. As a mentor, you have to have patience. Sometimes we rush things and our expectancy level of other people is unrealistic. We want them to match who we are. We are all different. As my mom once said, being different doesn't make you wrong, it just makes you different. We are dealing now with the generational issues. When I go into a company and talk about generations, the X-er's, and now the Y-generation, talk about all this. I think if you are going to be a great mentor today, you need patience.

The next characteristic that comes to mind is vulnerability. I think that there has to be an authenticity about yourself when you are going to be a mentor to someone else. In order to build that relationship, they need to know you've been there, done that, bought the t-shirt, a couple of key chains, and own a couple of bumper stickers. You have to be a person they believe in, not necessarily for what you've become but for who you are. I think for me it has been the most important characteristic in mentoring my children, Stephen, Josh, and Courtney. I try to be vulnerable. I say, "Listen, I know what you are going through and here is why." Then I give them an example from my life where I made a similar choice, and they look at me kind of like "Wow! Dad went through that too."

The other characteristic that is so important is believability. As mentioned earlier, do your actions match your beliefs? Here's something else I always attribute to my mom. She said, "Don't try to teach values to your children, because values aren't taught, values are caught." Because I believe that—I think to be a great mentor you have to be believable, and your believability is such that you really are a person that you look at and they model their actions after and say, "I want to be like that person." Before you can turn somebody loose, you have to make sure that they see something in you that they want and need.

So I think the three things would be patience, vulnerability, and believability. Maybe the best way of saying it is, Are you a person others would want to follow?

Wright

It's been said that great leaders have great vision. As the founder and CEO of your own company, do you believe that all great leaders have great vision?

Gilliland

I believe leadership and vision go together. I believe to be a great leader you have to have vision. But I think, for me, when I look at vision, there are some leaders that have great vision but have a less than stellar approach to people. I truly believe that great vision with mediocre people produces mediocre results. One of the things I've done with the business that I founded is that I hired people for who they were. I think one of the problems we have in today's business world is that we hire people for what they know and eventually have to fire them for who they are. I believe leaders need vision, and great leaders have it; but I believe that sometimes, no pun intended, we lose sight of it because we don't focus on people.

An example is the staff I've assembled at Performance Plus. My oldest son, Stephen, works at our business and is a great example. He has an incredible heart, an incredible passion. He is learning the skills and has no experience. I can teach him the skills and he can gain the experience, but I can't teach him attitude. You can't teach honesty. You can reference it and maybe model it, but you can't teach it. I think that is where I am at with leaders and vision. I think all great leaders have vision; but beyond vision, it takes the right motive and the right heart and good people. As I said, and it bears repeating, great vision with mediocre people produces mediocre results. You have to have great people. I know that Marsha and several other people that work with the business are those kind of people. We hired them for who we they are, not for what they know.

Wright

Most people are fascinated with the new TV shows about being a survivor. What has been the greatest comeback you have made from adversity in your career or life?

Gilliland

Wow.

Wright

That many, huh?

Gilliland

The greatest comeback I've ever made took twenty-one years. When I was eighteen, I left the confines of a loving mother who taught me right from wrong and reared me in a good Christian home. For twenty-one years I tried to do everything on my own without regard to the values and principles I had been taught. I strayed from a belief system that was centered on God and the right things. I didn't follow the Golden Rule and wasn't sure what being a father or husband was all about. Having children never made me a father, and getting married never made me a husband. Then, at age thirty-nine, I realized that my life direction had taken me down a path of lies, deceit, and self-destruction. It was then that my comeback began.

Wright

So you were the co-author of "The Prodigal Son"?

Gilliland

I'm not sure I co-authored it as much as I uniquely followed its story line. I really believe that the greatest comeback I ever made was the day I woke up and didn't like what I saw in the mirror. I began to realize that all the adversity I was facing was a result of Steve making the wrong choices. My advice for anyone reading this is to always remember that you make the choices and create your own reality and your own destiny. For me, I had created a destiny for almost twenty-one years where every time I found myself in a bad situation, I looked for somebody to blame. I now realize that every situation I encounter is a result of my choices, and everything that negatively happens to me personally and professionally is not because of something my mom or dad failed to do while raising me. It wasn't what somebody else had done; it was the choices I had made. It is ironic that you asked that question. The thing I recognize is that I am still in the process of making that comeback. I think that I still have a long way to go. I will continue to get up every morning and pray that I make the right choices. I hope everybody that reads this understands that sometimes, in the comebacks we make, we could have avoided even having to make a comeback at all. Just remember, comebacks are only necessary when you leave where you should have been—as you said, the prodigal son returned, but he never would have had to return if he had never left.

Wright

If you could have a platform and tell our audience something you feel would help or encourage them, what would you say?

Gilliland

I would tell them to Enjoy the Ride™ and just be yourself. Don't let anyone else define who you are; set and live by your own expectations. I find it interesting that we tell people how tough it is to raise our children and how tough it is to be a child today with all the peer pressure. I find that humorous. I think adults need to listen to what we are telling our children. We as adults are under the same peer pressure. As I've told people, I used to keep up with the Joneses. Now I bring them down to my level because it is cheaper.

I think if we would just be ourselves, our lives would be so much simpler and we really would enjoy the true joy of life. My wife, Charlotte, said to me one time, "I like the smell of a paid car more than the smell of a new car." Her point was that what we drive shouldn't be determined by anything other than what we need, not what we want someone to see us in. My brother is a great example of a guy who has always been himself and enjoyed the ride. He works hard, is loyal to his family and friends, and has never tried to live up to anyone else's expectations. His three children, Heidi, Crystal and Brock, are balanced kids who love their mother, love their father, respect their neighbors and are good citizens. If we could just tell more people that you are going to do yourself a favor and everybody around you if you just spend more time being yourself. Stop trying to be something you are not. For twenty-one years I tried to be something that I wasn't. So the advice I give people now is just Enjoy the Ride™ and be yourself. Just be who you are. It makes the ride so much smoother.

Wright

Steve, we are at the end of our program. It has been great. I could talk to you all day.

Gilliland

I've really enjoyed it.

Wright

Steve Gilliland has been described as one of the most passionate, dynamic, and versatile speakers in the world. His keynote speeches cover a variety of useful topics and are delivered with humor, insight, and contagious energy. I think we have all caught your contagious energy today, Steve, and I really appreciate you being on *Mission Possible!*

Gilliland

Thank you very much for the opportunity, and I look forward to doing it again some day.

Steve Gilliland

Performance Plus

P.O. Box 4182

Pittsburgh, PA 15202

(412) 766-0806

Fax: (412) 766-8998

E-mail: steveg@performanceplus1.com